The United States is in a time of
business turmoil, experiencing intense
competition from other countries, an
increasing national debt, a lack of
ethical standards, and the loss of traditionally strong markets to foreign
companies. In this book, J.H.U. Brown
and Jacqueline Comola point out the
failures, survey the challenges, and
indicate possible solutions for these
economic and social problems by focusing on the weaknesses in education that
have added so greatly to them. The loss
of excellence in American education,
Brown and Comola point out, crosses
all boundaries, from the college student,
to the manager and worker, to the general public. All must be re-educated in
their approaches toward business for
the United States to regain world
leadership.

The book focuses on a number of intertwined issues in business and education,
providing general examples of problems
followed by suggestions for effective
yet inexpensive solutions. Deficiencies
in management are addressed through
such topics as the failure of managers
to be aware of technology and its
impact, the inability to recognize the
need for quality, and the failure to stimulate the work force to greater productivity. School systems are faulted for
their incapacity to train students
properly in the lower grades, control
costs in such areas as medical care, and
fully exploit innovation. Following the
discussion of these and similar subjects,
a set of four chapters offer some effective proposals for change in the areas
of productivity, executive/worker inter-
action, management, and promoting
quality. With its applications in education, business, and technology, this
book will be an important resource for

Educating for Excellence

Educating for Excellence

IMPROVING QUALITY AND PRODUCTIVITY IN THE 90's

J.H.U. BROWN
AND
JACQUELINE COMOLA

AUBURN HOUSE
New York • Westport, Connecticut • London

Library of Congress Cataloging-in-Publication Data

Brown, J.H.U. (Jack Harold Upton).
    Educating for excellence : improving quality and productivity in
the 90's / J.H.U. Brown and Jacqueline Comola.
        p.   cm.
    Includes bibliographical references (p.   ) and index.
    ISBN 0-86569-030-8 (alk. paper)
    1. Education—Economic aspects—United States. 2. Working class—
Education—United States. 3. Industrial productivity—United
States. 4. Medical care—United States. 5. Educational change—
United States. I. Comola, Jacqueline. II. Title.
LC66.B76 1991
370.11'0973—dc20   90-22298

British Library Cataloguing in Publication Data is available.

Library of Congress Catalog Card Number: 90-22298
ISBN: 0-86569-030-8

First published in 1991

Auburn House, 88 Post Road West, Westport, CT 06881
An imprint of Greenwood Publishing Group, Inc.

Printed in the United States of America

The paper used in this book complies with the
Permanent Paper Standard issued by the National
Information Standards Organization (Z39.48-1984).

10 9 8 7 6 5 4 3 2 1

Copyright Acknowledgments

Grateful acknowledgment is given for permission to reprint material from the
following copyrighted sources:

Managing Innovation, © 1988 by the National Academy of Sciences, National
Academy Press, Washington, D.C.

Managing Microcomputers in Large Organizations, © 1985 by the National
Academy of Sciences.

Contents

vi   *Contents*

Tables and Figures

Preface

It sometimes appears there is a deliberate effort on the part of the American people to discourage excellence. We produce goods of poor quality, and we are losing ground in research and development. We do not encourage excellence in the public schools and as a result lag behind most of the developed countries of the world in the education of the young. We boast about our medical care system; yet, we are almost at the bottom of the list of developed and some undeveloped countries in infant mortality rates. Our crime rate exceeds that of most other countries and we have become a drug culture. We are in a time of business turmoil.

On the one hand there is intense and ever increasing competition from countries that American business would have regarded with contempt a few years ago. On the other hand, there are worrying signs of problems in the economy with increasing national debt and failure of foreign countries to meet debt obligations. This has been coupled with the lack of ethical standards in the community evidenced by the many Wall Street criminal prosecutions for stock fraud, cheating in the schools, and lack of public morality in government.

The inability to compete on an equal footing with foreign imports, in electronics and autos in particular, has been blamed on a variety of factors including cost of labor and cost of materials. No one has stepped forward to state that a large part of the blame is due to the poor management of American business and education—a loss of excellence. Yet the manager in business, government, or education is responsible for all of these factors and that is the thesis of this book.

The basis of economic development and excellence is education and the student from preschool through college must be prepared to meet the challenges of competition, managers must revise their approach to business and technology, the workers must become a part of the industrial enterprise rather than drawing from it by working only for money, and the public must learn to define excellence in terms of the environment as well as income or purchasing power.

We, as a people, are facing a cultural revolution in the age of technology. New methods of doing business, of performing simple tasks, and of using our resources are required and these methods can be learned only through education of the population as a whole.

There is much talk about adoption of the quality circle methods so well exploited in Japan, the revision of curriculum in the schools and the development of ethical standards in Congress and the country, all of which indicates that the United States must face reality and change if the country is to progress in the face of foreign imports and the challenges to education, medical care, and other areas of life. And the change must be implemented with a whole hearted cooperation of all concerned. Something must be done and done quickly or we will lose all except the service industries which contribute nothing to the economy.

All of these factors are intertwined. Without education we cannot produce workers who can compete in a era of high technology. If we cannot develop an educational system that will meet the future needs of the country, we will be a second rate power in the next decades. In other words, there is a challenge for excellence on all fronts and we are doing little to face up to the requirements. We will attempt in this book to survey the challenges, indicate possible solutions, and point out our failures across the broad front of our economy and social system. We have selected several major areas of attack and will concentrate on those although we could as easily have selected others with equal impact.

The health care system is a major part of our total economy and is one of the most inefficient management and educational operations of both government and industry, so must be discussed. Examining the environmental impact of many of the things we do and questioning the directions we are going to clean up the air and water are major tasks. The educational system is in chaos, and the young are not being trained to provide value to the economy of the future.

But harping on the ills of our society would be of no value unless we had some suggestions for change. And some changes are occurring, albeit very slowly. We have picked out a number of specific but representative examples of change which could be accelerated without undue expense. Most of these are concerned with overall improvement in management, style and relationships but serve to demonstrate that change is possible.

J.H.U.Brown
Jacqueline Comola

Abbreviations

AI	Artificial Intelligence
ATI	Applied Technology Initiative
APQC	American Productivity and Quality Center
ASQC	American Society for Quality Control
BLS	Boston Latin School
CAD/CAM	Computer Assisted Design and Manufacturing
CAT	Computerized Axial Tomography
CEO	Chief Executive Officer
CIT	Center for Innovative Technology
CMI	Computer Managed Instruction
COL	Cost of Living
DRAM	Dynamic Random Access Memory
EEC	European Economic Community
FMME	Fund For Multinational Management Education
FPA	Flexible Production Automation
GAO	Government Accounting Office
GM	General Motors
GNP	Gross National Product
HALO	Handling Alarms Using Logic
IESC	International Executive Service Corps
JUSE	Japanese Union of Scientists and Engineers
LDC	Lesser Developed Countries
MIS	Management Information System
MITI	Ministry of International Trade and Industry (Japan)
MNR	Magnetic Nuclear Resonance
NACQ	National Advisory Council on Quality
NAE	National Academy of Engineering
NAS	National Academy of Sciences

NIST	National Institute for Standards and Technology
NRC	National Research Council
PC	Personal Computer
PET	Positron Emission Tomography
QC	Quality Circle
R and D	Research and Development
RFP	Request for Proposal
SRC	Semiconductor Research Corporation
TASP	Texas Academic Skills Program
TC	Total Control (Japanese system)
TQC	Total Quality Control (Japanese system)
VAR	Variance Analysis Report
VCR	Video Cassette Recorder
VITA	Volunteers in Technical Assistance

Educating for Excellence

1

Introduction

As this book is written, the United States is being outclassed by most of the other industrial nations of the world. We are being outperformed by Japan, Sweden, Germany, France, and others in technology and production. One of the reasons is that the American workers' attitude can be identified as 'money first and foremost'. It will take a greater appreciation on our part of the problems of industry to understand future developments, or the lack of them, if the United States is to remain an industrial power.[1]

The Japanese method of national development subjugates the aims of the individual to the needs of the state, within reason, while the American worker does not work to world class standards of output because of lack of education, motivation, and skills (Table 1-1).[2] This has been clearly demonstrated in the area of technology where United States' foreign trade has gone from a surplus export of technology of more than $20 billion in 1980 to a deficit export of about $3 billion in 1986, and the gap is widening.[3] The technology under development overseas is in such vital areas as computer chips, microprocessors, and communications. American business talks glibly of technology, but sees it only as a means to further immediate profit. We also fail to understand that technology may decrease rather than increase productivity, as has been clearly demonstrated in medicine where technology has only increased the cost of care without markedly increasing cure rates.

Further statistics can be added. If the real wages are measured in merchandise shipped overseas, our economy must be rethought. We need to educate business leaders that we now live in a one-world economy as a industrial complex and America must be able to act competitively in the world in order to survive. An indication of attitude is revealed by a questionnaire sent to executives regarding the problems they face in trading in foreign markets and the reasons for the large trade deficit. Only 15 percent thought American products were inferior, and only

6 percent thought quality and price were a factor in competition in foreign markets. This reflects a gross misunderstanding of the role of American business in the world economy, and a more important point, the role of quality in producing goods which will be salable both at home and abroad to a more sophisticated consumer.

Table 1-1

Indices of technological development in Japan, West Germany and the United States with progress in each country. Figures are rounded on same base year.

Indices	Japan	W. Ger.	U.S	Measurement
GNP	135	115	105	% Increase since 1960
Labor Costs	115	120	152	% Increase since 1960
R and D expenditure	45	65	70	% Increase since 1960
Plant Installations	25	15	12	Percent GNP
R and D-Nondefense	3	3	2	Percent of GNP
Infrastructure	4	1.7	0.2	Percent of GNP
Graduate degrees	23	6	26	Percent of college grads
Grads in Science	27	34	20	Percent of graduates
Days in school	243	190	180	Per academic year
Days lost by labor	163	0	4,417	Days lost by strikes
Patents Issued	8-21	9-1	67-53	Percent of patents- 1978 and 1988

The major problem is assumed to be an unequal playing field despite the fact that American are buying Japanese goods and cars at an ever increasing rate. All consumer surveys suggest foreign goods are considered to be superior in quality. This stigma on American industry must be removed.[4] To some extent the blinders have been removed. Some industries are beginning to develop standards of quality as opposed to quantity, new warranty programs are being developed for major products, and there are a few vague indications that the negative trade balance is improving, depending on actions in the Middle East, and our exports are slowly increasing. The American public has been educated to quality but American business must be similarly oriented to quality-made articles, which clearly suggests the blinders must be removed through education.

Second, business (industry, health care, etc.) is unwilling to face the facts of low productivity. The attitude can be summarized with two examples. At a recent board meeting in the United States a paraphrased report went as follows: "We lost $20 million last year and will have to close three plants and lay off two thousand workers. However, the management feels it has done a good job and will provide raises of $50,000 each for the top executives." In a company in Japan: "We lost 200 million yen. This is obviously the fault of poor management and therefore the managers will take a 35 percent pay cut. However, we will not lay off workers although each may have to take a 5 percent cut." The contrast is obvious. Other contrasts can also be made. This attitude of workers and bosses in America contributes to the problem.

The very title of a famous book on the corporate executive, *The View from the 20th Floor,* expresses exactly the isolation of the American executive from the workers. The Japanese executive, on the other hand, sits at one desk in a large office. There is no twentieth floor. Again the contrast is apparent. Business extols the productivity of the American worker as the highest in the world in the range of $33,000 per capita but this does not reflect real efficiency. The Japanese require about 100 hours to produce a car that is almost fault-free, while the American work force requires 180 hours to assemble a car that has hundreds of defects. This is the fault of management and poor education and training of the workers. We have not trained workers to make excellence a first priority. In fact a recent poll of CEOs found 36 percent considered financial arrangements to be paramount while only 5 percent considered quality as an important element of the job. In contrast the Japanese worker is trained to consider quality to be the first priority and to understand the entire process of manufacture and how the methods adopted affect quality. The results could have been anticipated. We are losing our share of the world market to the Japanese and the European.[4] Karmin [5] estimates 66 percent of all radios and televisions, 63 percent of shoes, 45 percent of machine tools, 28 percent of automobiles, and 25 percent of all computers in the United States are imported from foreign sources (Fig. 1-1).

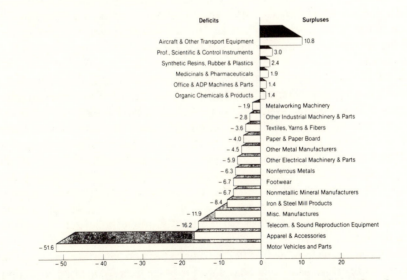

Fig. 1-1. United States trade balances demonstrating the loss in many markets (Taken from *Technological Dimensions of International Competitiveness*. Washington, D.C: National Academy Press, 1988.)

The response of the managers to the loss of the market is not to do excellent work, it is to shout for a level playing field and higher tariffs so the inefficient American can compete with the more efficient Korean, Chinese, Japanese, or European. We may complain that the American worker is paid much more than counterparts in other countries and this may be true (although not in real terms as indicated above), but the manager has set no example. An American executive makes about twenty times the average salary of workers in yearly income while in other countries the spread is only about five times. There is no wonder the worker clamors for more pay and is not concerned about productivity. [3]

We must turn our educational system around. Since 1979 the employment in the computer industry has increased 44 percent, and in electronics 26 percent, while it has decreased 51 percent in steel making and 15 percent in automobile assembly line operations. Clearly our educational system must be oriented toward a more technological training. In a technological world quality not quantity must be the hallmark of production, and this can be achieved only through education.

America suffers in comparison with most of the developed world in this regard. This is a tragic circumstance when we realize quality control was invented by an American, W.E. Deming, and exported to Japan only after it was not adopted in the United States.

When asked, 57 percent of Americans say that they believe the reason that more goods are being bought overseas is American goods are of poor quality. This is blamed on the workers and only to a small extent on the managers. Actually, the reverse is true. Managers must be blamed for not stimulating quality control, for not increasing productivity, for failing to motivate workers and for accepting shoddy work output. And most of all for not providing proper training in these areas.

To create a turnaround, we must examine each of the facets of the reasons for inefficiency and poor production and determine how each can be polished to better efficiency. Much depends upon education. We can begin by apologizing for the frequent mention of Japan as both competitor and example in this book. American business has been obsessed with Japan and its increasing control of world markets for the past several years, and is therefore interested in the Japanese method of management. Furthermore, Japan offers the best example of many of the points we wish to make. As one example, investments by Japan in the United States have grown from a few billion dollars ten years ago to more than $31 billion dollars last year. [6] If the portfolio investments are added, the total is more than $200 billion.

This is not all bad. Some 300,000 jobs have been created directly as a result of the Japanese effort. More than that, Japan is passing on some of its educational and training ideas in factories set up in the United States in cooperation with American manufacturers, and they serve as excellent examples of many of the points we will make.

We will use many examples of technology in this book; the reasons are apparent. All industry and in fact all society depends upon and uses technology daily. The problems of the computer age, the automation of industry, and the development of new materials and methods are rooted in technological advances. Modern executives must also be technocrats or they are not likely to last long in our society. Finally, technology education is lagging in the United States and it must be stimulated if we are to compete. Our students are leaving high school without a scientific background and with no grounding in mathematics. Of greater importance for the future is the relationship of America as a whole to global strategies of other countries.

U.S. students are unable to compete with the students in several foreign countries who are likely to be leaving school and entering the job market. When the average American high school student cannot locate a country on a world map or understand why certain products are produced in given locations, we enter the global arena at a disadvantage. As Duchêne has pointed out, the international markets are set within a societal makeup and any changes must be reflected in a change in the society.[9] As an example, the changes in the Soviet Union as a result of *perestroika* are rapidly changing the world as it looks toward new markets. We must develop the leadership in management we do not now have. As Packard has stated, "good research, no matter how brilliantly executed, without engineering skills and trained workers is an absolute waste of corporate assets."[7]

COMPETITIVENESS

Americans have adopted a unique approach to business. Business attitudes have changed from high quality production of small numbers of items in the day of the individual craftsman to high finance and corporate structure as opposed to better production standards and better training of workers. Profits are obtained by corporate raiding rather than production. Lee Iacocca has said: "I can make more money by trading in money than by manufacturing cars," and the result is apparent in the auto industry. When United States Steel surrendered the steel business in favor of a variety of other industries, the point was driven home. Many students of the field say such money trading does nothing to improve the economy and, if too much attention is focused on the process, it will result in lower productivity of industry as a whole. As we will point out again, the fault lies with managers who are not trained in processes of an industry but in the exploitation of money. This attitude reveals much about our inability to compete in the world marketplace.

But the fault is not entirely in industry. The buyer and the citizen share the blame for our failures in competition. Competition, as we shall explore later, depends on innovation and development, and the funds are not available because of the poor saving habits of the American people. David Gergen pointed out last year, we saved about 3 percent of after-tax income, while the Germans saved 12 percent and the Japanese saved about 17 percent of their income. These funds are available for investment in plants and equipment. As a result the Japanese, with half our population living on islands the size of California, are adding more new development and infrastructure each year than is the entire American economy. No wonder we cannot compete.

Such problems are also reflected in the trend toward the service industries. Services, whether in fast food suppliers or medical treatment, are rapidly dominating the industrial market. And this represents a major shift in society and a decrease in productivity. When we were at the height of production in the heavy industries (during the Second World War, for example), moving a worker into a service area decreased productivity about 5 percent. Now the movement of a worker into a service position decreases his/her productivity by up to 40 percent. And this trend is exaggerated by the enormous bureaucracy built up by the industrial giants and by the educational and health care systems. The supernumerary staff adds nothing to output but adds significantly to the costs of the product. Services accounted for 86 percent of all jobs created in 1984 and the ratio is steadily increasing. Recent data indicate 50 percent of all workers are now office workers, and therefore only 50 percent of the working force actually contributes to our productivity. As we shall see, industry, in using more low skill service positions, effectively prevents the overall development that could improve productivity.

The usual claim is that technology through automation of the office will restore the balance, reduce the office work force, and improve productivity, but the evidence does not suggest that such is the case. According to the Bureau of Labor Statistics (BLS), white-collar employment is actually rising steadily while blue-collar workers are falling in numbers. In fact the situation is so bad the BLS has decided it will no longer report employment in separate categories because the information is so skewed. One of the reasons may be that the productivity of the white-collar worker is falling. The use of consultants, lawyers, and other specialists by industry absorbs hours of work time, involves millions of dollars, and contributes nothing to our economy except their salaries.

There are some steps that could be taken to restore excellence to the marketplace. Some major procedures are anathema to the white-collar workers, but may be necessary to meet worldwide competition.

1. Reduce the number of steps in the hierarchy to four or five by laying off 50 percent of the administrative staffs and reeducate the remainder.

2. Pay only on achievements in productivity.

3. Equip executives with word processors and computers and require them to do their own work to improve technological efficiency.

4. Reduce accounting demands to actual needs (accounting is a defensive measure and much of it is not necessary to run a business).

5. Find new sources of growth in industry.
6. Examine the capital-labor ratio.

At one time it was less expensive to substitute machines (capital) for labor but now machines are growing more and more expensive, and the reverse may be true. Japan is using labor-intensive methods to lead the world in productivity.

Each of these steps requires reeducation of the executive, the work force, and the public. We must be prepared to start in the lower grades and revise our curriculum through college in order to compete with a better educated work force in other countries. We can end this chapter in no better way than to paraphrase the editorial in *U.S. News and World Report* for December 6, 1989, by Mortimer Zuckerman:

> By the 1990s we will no longer be the most affluent nation. The ECC will have 350 million affluent customers.
> We are being out competed. It took the United States thirty years to become the richest country in the world. It has taken the Japanese just five. The richest banks in the world are Japanese, the real estate in Tokyo alone is worth more than the entire state of California, the ECC has 40 percent of college graduates majoring in science, we have 16 percent. In the 1970's we generated about 70 percent of all technology and innovation. This year we will generate only about 33 percent and most is for the military. Ten years ago we faced competition in some 5 percent of our goods sold within the country. This year the figure will be 75 percent.

We hear the old cliché of "one world", but one world encompasses more than geography. We are one world with respect to education of the work force, need for technology, international trade, governmental policy and business. Adjustments must be made in American business to reflect the concept.

REFERENCES

1. S. Brooks, "Giving More to the Have Nots," *Insight,* March 27, 1989, p. 28.
2. T. J. Murrin, "Thinking Globally, Acting Nationally," *Issues in Science and Technology* 6 (4):50 (Summer 1990).
3. S. Ramo, *Regaining Leadership through Industrial R and D.* Washington, D.C.: National Academy of Engineering Reports, December 1987.
4. National Academy of Engineering, *The Technological Dimensions of International Competitiveness.* Washington, D.C.: National Academy Press, 1988.
5. M. W. Karmin et al., "Will the U.S. Stay Number One?" *U.S. News and World Report,* February 2, 1987, p. 18.
6. L. Thurow, "A Weakness in Process Technology," *Science* 238:1659 (1987).

7.   G. Packard, "Partners in Prosperity," *Atlantic Monthly,* January 1988, p. 41.

8.   D. Halberstam, *The Reckoning.* New York: Avon Press, 1987.

9.   F. Duchêne and G. Shepherd, *Managing Industrial Change in Western Europe.* New York: Frances Pinter, 1987.

2

Technology, Education, and Business

The cumbersome response of the American economy makes for slow change, and when this is coupled with the resistance of many organizations, any change is likely to be a long time coming. This is especially true in the area of technology. Yet technology is now the key to excellence. The newer technologies save time and personnel, reduce costs, and improve the product in every area except health care. But a successful effort in technology use requires a major research and development effort. Development of products, use of robots, and other applications, all require research and development (R and D) efforts on a large scale. Technological devices affect performance of employees in the workplace and technical communications must increase if we are to compete.

The management of R and D will be a major effort in the future. Unfortunately it has not been so in the immediate past. The major revolutions in manufacturing, education, and agriculture all required new technology in the past, and a new technology must be found for future development.

Past experience dictates that although a company may have a large staff engaged in R and D, only the managers and the top 5 percent of the staff will make the major contributions, but they set the tone for the entire organization.[1] The rest of the R and D staff members are largely pairs of hands that can carry out directives but will contribute little to the advancement of science. Upper echelons must be recognized, nourished, and encouraged if technology is to advance.

Any new technologies such as biotechnology, genetics, and new methods of forming structures require that business, science, and quality control be mixed together in a totally new way.[2] The proper training for the manager of technology will not be found in the conventional business school staffed largely by Ph.D.'s in business. They are specialists in their fields and specialists are not very competent at cutting across disciplines in science along with knowledge in trading and the law that comprises the area of technology.

The rapid development of technology may serve to introduce a new style of management. Although MBAs have been increasing steadily in number and some 70,000 per year are now awarded, the old style of management by the numbers may be outworn. The new focus must be on entrepreneurship if business is to survive foreign competition. Foreign competition also means that the manager must be proficient in foreign languages, and in developing productivity in competition with foreign firms.[3],[4] The United States has not been outstanding in this regard.

Reports from the American Association of Business Schools which accredits programs in the universities, show the schools are providing quantitative management skills at the expense of broad management techniques. But the wise business schools are already changing the curriculum. MIT has developed a management-engineering joint program to study organizations and productivity. Others are stressing the need for production of quality products in contrast to the mass production standard that has been the cornerstone of American business. As an example of the change, Lester Thurow, dean of MIT Business School, says, "You can't use numbers to make a decision such as to switch to powdered metal technology from conventional methods." Such a major change involves machines, people, and technology in a mix that can't be duplicated in an accounting area.[5] The young executive has not been taught to manage R and D and therefore technology, while his older counterpart was not exposed to the world of computers, laser communications, and interactive networks and is equally lost.

One part of the problem is the large salaries and commissions paid to brokers and money managers on Wall Street that attract the service oriented young MBA. Once the present active market fades, and there is every indication it will, we may see more managers forced onto the factory floor without sufficient training or expertise. It has been estimated Wall Street will lose some 50,000 positions in money management within the next few years, and most of those who will lose jobs are not equipped for positions in heavy industry or production. There is also the question of the need for so many MBAs. Japan with a bustling economy and one that outproduces our own, awards 70 business degrees per year from its one business school, one one-thousandth of the number graduated in the United States.

One of the reasons why Japanese business excels is the way the young executive is trained. Typically a new graduate enters a firm and for several years spends six months or longer in each of the various departments of the company learning the business from the bottom up. He is then assigned to one department but may be reassigned at any time.[6] He knows he will advance at the same rate as his fellow graduates, and if he is exceptional, may be selected for higher executive training. The United States business schools, backed by desires of companies, have typically taken the position that a young man (or woman) should be trained intensively in one operation and have only a perfunctory knowledge of the rest of the business world. This tends to segregate industry into parcels with great substantive knowledge in one sector but little overall knowledge of the entire operation. As a result the CEO usually comes to head a diverse business with few skills in overall management. The Japanese CEO, on the other hand, has a varied knowledge of the entire company and its long term objectives.

Much of the above discussion has roots in the ability to compete. As we know, today's newspapers are continually bombarded with complaints from the manufacturers about the level playing field. The old argument, advanced in this book, says other countries dump goods on the market at prices below production costs, they support manufactured goods that are just entering a market, and they cooperate with industry in developing markets. The solution, so the story goes, is to place tariffs on such goods to raise the price to compete with American goods and then to force the countries engaging in such practice to open markets to American goods.

The reverse argument is equally telling. The Americans, so say the Germans and the English, the Japanese and the Koreans, suffer from several problems. Productivity is low so that the cost of production is high, making goods prohibitively expensive in foreign markets. Second, the quality is poor so that most people will not buy the goods at any price. Finally, the American work force has it too good, with too many perks, too little demand by the managers for quality and productivity, and too much guaranteed income so that work standards are low.

The answer does not lie in cutting costs at the expense of quality. The best example is the classic problem affecting the costs of medical care in the United States. There is no question but that the cost of health care is too high, and there is no question but that certain innovations can reduce costs without sacrifice of quality.[7] The development of health maintenance organizations (HMOs) in industry to provide for the health care of workers without allowing great freedom of choice in order to reduce high costs is a case in point. The problem is to adjust cost and quality simultaneously to optimize both. This may also be the dilemma of American industry as a whole.

An example of our poor methods is the semiconductor industry.[8] The United States lost a commanding lead in the field in just ten years. In 1975 Americans had 90 percent of the market in dynamic random access memory (DRAM) chips but by 1986 the Japanese had 90 percent of the market. The semiconductors are vital for the military, for manufacturing, and for installation in consumer goods that account for 15 percent of the GNP. At the moment the United States is considered two years behind the Japanese in semiconductor technology.

Much of the loss in the semiconductor technology market has often been attributed to two factors: the loss of entrepreneurial spirit and the failure to cooperate. Many small companies sprang up with an inventive genius at their head and went into direct competition with all other similar companies. The skills in invention were not matched by skills in marketing and pricing, while the Japanese on the other hand organized a highly integrated governmental, industrial complex and rapidly absorbed information and technology from around the world.

Excellence is also lost in other ways. The long-term outlook of the Japanese government and related industry cannot be matched in this country. In fact a long-term policy is a real detriment to a company in the United States. When Martin-Marietta announced a long term R and D plan for regaining lost markets, its stock fell $8 a share. [9] True, the American profits on a short-term basis are about twice those of the typical Japanese company, but this is of little benefit in the long run if the product cannot compete.

The semiconductor industry has begun to adopt some of the Japanese cooperative system, and it may be paying off. Eleven companies formed the Research Corporation in 1982 for a cooperative research effort. By 1986 there were thirty-five companies contributing $18 million to a variety of research projects with some $2.5 million contributed by the U.S. government. [10] Interestingly enough, the United States as a whole probably contributes more to semiconductor R and D than do the Japanese, but the Japanese manage their funds better and avoid the duplication that is the plague of the United States industry. Most of our R and D in semiconductors is done in small plants with few personnel led typically by a single individual who is a genius in the field. This individual as a rule is not highly competent in business and cannot exploit his inventions readily. Excellence in R and D does not lead to excellence in production.

Similar methods could be adapted by other industries, and in fact, we are seeing the first bloom of the idea. Chrysler has signed an agreement with a Korean firm to produce cars in the United States, and Ford has a similar agreement with Japanese firms. Other arrangements include European firms. It is unfortunate that the combination represents overseas firms rather than a consortium of American companies. Japan has done better. Some years ago Mazda introduced a new car with a rotary engine. The engine had problems, and Mazda elected to withdraw it from the market. It was able to buy replacement engines from Nissan and other Japanese manufacturers at below market price to put into Mazdas until their engine was corrected. We are not likely to see a similar arrangement in the United States.

Our economy is rapidly developing a manufacturing strategy based on deindustrialization. The United States is losing its capacity for industrial expansion in high technology industry because much of the production is overseas. Other considerations must enter the equation. While it is true the workers in Mexico or Central America earn one dollar an hour compared to the United States workers' ten dollars an hour, the turnover of workers, the lack of education, and the lack of understanding of machinery must also be taken into consideration. The end result is a fine trade off between greater flexibility at home and cheaper costs overseas. We shall explore this topic more fully in a later chapter.

Finally, as we move industry overseas, the standard of living in those countries rises, wage demands increase, and the profitability gap between the country and the United States decreases. Japan began by providing cheap labor to outproduce the worker in the United States and is now finding that as its wages increase, Taiwan is moving into the gap with low-cost labor and taking markets from the Japanese as they took markets from us. And the cycle will continue. China may outcompete Taiwan in the near future although we have to await the outcome of the latest upheaval to make a final determination.

Some industries have begun to recognize the problems. Some fifty or more consortia have been formed between academia and industry, often with governmental participation, to encourage excellence in American products by rapidly developing ideas from basic research and by encouraging the university to work on problems closely related to quality of industrial output.

These examples indicate that we are seeing some development of the technological-educational-industrial complex that is so well established in Japan and in Europe. Studies indicate that the rate of return of technological and R and D expenditures is very high indeed.[11] However, a National Academy of Sciences (NAS) study on manufacturing concluded that the narrow view of manufacturing of making a single element that is then combined with other single elements, each with its own standards, to finally produce a finished product with the sum of all of the errors built into the system must be abandoned in favor of a system of integrated elements that mitigates against compartmentalization[9] (Fig. 2-1).

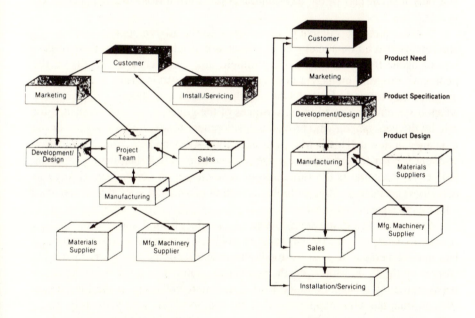

Product Realization Process   **Traditional Organization and Procedures**

Fig. 2-1. Comparison of the usual manufacturing methods with the new processes (From *Technological Dimensions of International Competitiveness.* Washington, D.C.: National Academy Press, 1988.)

In addition, the American managers with business school backgrounds have not learned to manage technology well, largely because of the way they are trained.

Squires cites a classic example.[12] Managers designed a perfect rifle for the armed forces, the M-16. Never having been in combat, they knew little of the technology processes and behavior under such conditions and four years of tinkering with the design were required to produce a working weapon. Research might well have prevented the problems in the first place. The military is notorious for the development of ideas without the excellence in research to exploit innovation and produce a complete product. All military equipment requires years of tinkering before it is suited for combat. Missiles that do not work, planes that do not meet specifications, and tanks that cannot fire accurately have all been cited by Congress and others as a failure of quality control. The frequent abandonment of projects (the mobile antiaircraft gun) indicates the lack of scientific planning and organization.

The causes are deep rooted. In a complex organization like today's industrial giants or the government there are failures of communication from one source to another. Part of the problem is the overlying layers of bureaucracy and the failure of communication between ranks. Of course, this comes back to the statement that only a small part of the information is transferred from the manager to the worker.

There is a major problem of incest between the government and industry in our country that automatically tends to decrease efficiency. Steady flows of personnel occur from industry to government and vice versa, especially in the Pentagon. Program managers in the military transfer to industry to manage the program they formerly funded. Under such circumstances, there is little wonder a weapon system developed under auspices of the government will be pushed for sale by the very person who provided development funds and now works for the industry making it. This is a form of education—the industry educates the government worker to respond to the needs of industry rather than the needs of the public. An example is the formation of political action committees (PACs) so that large sums can be directed to the reelection of a Congressional representative who favors a particular position.

Closely related to the development of a product from R and D is the bane of American enterprise, the bureaucracy. It has been estimated by researchers that less than 48 percent of what the top management really intends ever reaches the worker on the floor. Moreover, the smaller the number of levels of supervisors between the top manager and the worker, the more consistent is the final result. We can imagine what happens at General Motors (GM) with sixteen levels of corporate management. Little or no information probably reaches the worker. R and D developed on lower levels that might make a major change in business productivity may never reach the top management.

In contrast, the typical Japanese company has only four levels of supervision. The end result is clearly displayed in a Reuters dispatch of August 24, 1987, where the Ford Motor Company complained that the Japanese were producing equivalent automobiles *in* the United States using United States workers and many American materials at $800 per car less than the American company could produce a similar product.[13] Ford argued not to increase managerial talent to produce a cheaper car with better quality, but to use the information as a ploy to drive down wage demands by unions. While it may be true that wages paid by Ford may be more than those paid by the Japanese *in this country,* the differences cannot be great. In at least two major cases the automobile workers have rejected the United Automobile Workers (UAW) position in favor of the Japanese style, certainly suggesting worker satisfaction. Rather, management practices should be more closely examined. For example, the workers in the Japanese factory contribute ideas related to R and D to improve the product; most of these reach senior management, and many are implemented with resulting savings to the company and rewards to the worker.

The difference is clearly indicated by the Japanese handling of the introduction of robots into plants. The Japanese found that it required great management skill to introduce robots into its plants. A high degree of discipline and standardized work procedures on the production floor were necessary. Robots are only as successful as the working environment in which they are placed, and an inefficient plant produces only inefficient robot operations. The choice is a technical one. There is little use in introducing a complex robot to do a simple operation or one that can be done cheaper and easier by a human. American managers simply ordain that robots will be introduced and the employees take the consequences. This single example illustrates a world of difference between Japanese and American styles of management. Yet M. Fujisawa, founder of Honda, and a major developer of robotics, has said that despite these differences in American and Japanese management, the business management theory is about 95 percent the same, and yet, he adds carefully, differs in *all* important respects.[14] The Japanese have attempted to solve the man-machine interface, improve excellence of manufacture, and enhance quality control by the introduction of an old American business invention, the quality circle (QC). The basic idea lies in the Z-theory of W. Ouchi, which insists that the involved worker is the mainstay of any attempt at quality control and productivity.[15] The QC is a small group of workers with various kinds of expertise who work together to solve a problem. For example, the group may construct a complete car from start to finish without the typical assembly-line procedures. The group has the freedom to make changes in processes, alter rates of work, and take further steps in order to achieve the best possible results. Decisions are group decisions, and there are no real bosses although the most competent may be the leader.

The concept of participation is crucial to the operation of the theory. The American bureaucracy says to an employee, "We are paying you. Do what we say." The Japanese and the Z-theorist would say, "This is what we want to accomplish. Do you have any suggestions for how to get there?" In the Z-type company there are no superstars.[16] Everyone is part of the team, and the team efforts are recognized as the company effort. The introduction of QC or the Z-method into American automobile factories by the Japanese when they negotiated cooperative agreements with General Motors and others has improved company efforts. As we have repeated many times thus far, American technology is lagging behind the technology of other countries because we have not adopted these measures.

To some extent this is to be expected. High technology has always replaced a lower form throughout history. The Stone Age disappeared when bronze was discovered, and the Bronze Age vanished in the wake of the invention of steel. The high technology of today is a low technology product tomorrow, and this is reflected in the marketplace.

The United States has usually taken the attitude that we are ahead in technology and need not worry until the other countries catch up. The problem is that other countries do not know this and have not only caught up, in many instances they have surpassed the United States, and this is directly the fault of the managers of American business. In the words of the old pitcher, Satchel Paige, "Don't look behind—someone may be gaining on you." The American business person needs to look behind before he/she is passed.

A few examples will illustrate the thesis. No VCRs are being built in the United States although they were invented here. The multibillion dollar industry employing hundreds of thousands of workers is located entirely overseas. And the situation is getting worse.

Kodak has invented a minivideo camera with an almost unlimited market but it also is being made exclusively overseas. [2] The tape recorder was invented in the United States, but none are now made here. The same situation prevails in the machine tool industry. Today imports represent almost 40 percent of the entire market of machine tools in the United States and exports are almost zero. Yet only ten years ago we exported more tools than we imported.

CAD/CAM tools and designs are being imported by IBM from Sanyo Seiko. When General Motors (GM) asked for bids on new presses for automobile plants, the Japanese were the low bidders on all of them. Computers are another example. IBM has parts made in Taiwan and Korea, disk drives are made in Hong Kong, and the IBM PC is actually made in its entirety by Matsushita. Apple's printers are made in Japan.

As we have mentioned, one of the reasons is the reliability of the foreign products. The reliability of Japanese, Taiwanese, and European autos is well known, and there is no need to recap their success in the United States. Less well known is the fact that the nuclear reactors in Japan and France have less than one emergency shutdown per year while those in the United States average about five to six per year. American reactors operate about 50 to 60 percent of the time while the reactors in Japan operate 70 to 75 percent of the time. The return on investment is obvious.

There are other reasons for the success of the nuclear power industry elsewhere. The Japanese developed a new welding technology when it was found the reactors leaked because of the effect of high temperatures on welds; we have not yet adopted the technology.

One of the reasons for the Japanese success and also for success in other industrialized countries is the formation of a government-industrial complex.[9],[10] In Japan, the Ministry for International Trade and Industry (MITI), works closely with Japanese industry—too closely, many onlookers contend. The organization combines various companies into a concentrated thrust in world markets such as the takeover of the computer chip market mentioned above. It is said to finance start-up for new industry to compete on world markets and to encourage by a finance plan the dumping of materials on international markets. The same series of events is now occurring in Korea and Taiwan, and now the Japanese are complaining about the intense competition. In sum, we have not yet decided that we must compete in technology on an international scale with others of the same industrial rank. To do so will require that Americans develop new attitudes toward competitors, toward quality production methods, and toward better efficiency.

It has been said with more than a grain of truth that America leads the world in innovation.[10] Our R and D effort is one of the largest in the world and the number of international prizes won by Americans attests to the character of the work. Yet, it has also been said that if an American patents something today, next week the Japanese or the Taiwanese will be selling it on the streets of New York while the American is still looking for funds. This implies that while we are an innovative people, we do not have great productivity with respect to use of R and D. And this is the fault of industry.

Branscomb has pointed out in a speech to the National Academy of Engineering that cooperation between government and industry is essential to R and D.[10] Most governments wish to maintain a strong R and D and production capability in those industries in the national interest. This becomes difficult when foreign competition can produce better quality goods at a cheaper price.

We must learn to develop our innovations rapidly and efficiently to preserve the national interest and our own markets. One of the major problems is that the United States does not invest in R and D for the long haul. The vast majority of R and D funds are supplied by the military for specific projects related to weapons development. That other developed countries place large sums into R and D industrial research is the reason we see new techniques in heavy machinery production, metal smelting, and nuclear energy developed overseas and not in the United States.

Technology can be a cause of loss of innovative talent. The computerized checkout counters in our grocery stores require no mental ability on the part of the clerk, and the minute division of labor in technologically oriented offices discourages thinking on the part of the low-level, white-collar worker. The executive may be similarly stymied. The ready availability of data bases, projections, and organizational materials may lead to a stultification of ideas because these may sometimes be substituted for thought.

THE WORK FORCE IN A TECHNICAL SOCIETY

It is necessary to discuss the problems relating to personnel in several contexts because of the varied nature of employees and the tasks to which they are assigned. The basic theory will be discussed in a later chapter. Technical revolution is changing the work force and therefore industry and academia. Almost 60 percent of the work force will be white-collar workers by 1991 while the number of blue-collar workers has steadily declined and will continue to do so. This creates massive problems in productivity. The white-collar force generates no product and therefore does not contribute to the productivity of the nation or to the GNP. The enormous turnover of wealth on Wall Street through trading also contributes nothing to the GNP and productivity. The one exception may lie in the invention and sale of computer software.[16]

The computerization of offices also raises problems of quality control. The mindless division of labor into minute specific tasks to facilitate the use of machines forces boredom and dissatisfaction on workers. The end result may be loss of productivity. In addition, the mix of workers is changing. Within the last fifteen years the number of computer-related positions has increased some 40 times while the number of stenographers and typists has decreased by almost the same amount. The skilled worker with new tasks assigned on expensive machines requires supervision, and as a result the number of supervisors has increased 10 times in the same fifteen-year period.[15] There is now a new level of management and a new type of person to manage. In addition, the manager has not learned to use computers well. Of all offices, 50 percent now have a mainframe computer, but the number of office workers using personal computers is a little more than one-half that number. Less than 2 percent of executives have a personal computer or terminal at home and do any work there.

Despite the large number of computers in industry (Table 2-1) they are not well used. Eason found in a large corporation with 36 online computers, 5 of them did about 75 percent of the total work and half of them were almost never used.[17] He also discovered that most executives had computers on their desks, but most never used them or had secretaries or staff obtain the information. When we consider that most mainframe computers are used by only a small portion of the work force for bookkeeping purposes and data storage, it is apparent the personal use of computers by the executive is not large.

Additional information indicates 40 percent of managers consider the computer to be unfriendly or not suited to their needs and 81 percent claim that the computer does not improve performance of the organization. There are reasons for the problems. In order for a communications system to work in an organization it must be understood and appreciated by everyone.

Surveys have indicated that managers believe that the work force was brought early into the decision to implement a new technology, but the work force in the organization felt that they were not included, indicating a dichotomy of interest and information.[18] The lack of communications at this level precludes innovation and development of technology. Although there has been much talk of managerial workstations with computer terminals and other equipment, Bikson and Gutek found out that they were not very effective, bearing out the finding that the executives are not very computer literate.[18] Another proposition has been to supply the executive with error-free or risk-free systems of data base interrogation but this also has not proven to be feasible. We might sum up by saying with Bikson and Gutek that the relationship between computer capability and performance of corporations has not been proven.

Table 2-1

Companies with the largest number of computers

Company	Computers	% Networked	No. Employees
General Electric	40,000	100	200,000
Dupont	30,000	50	20,000
G T E	28,000	50	150,000
Hughes Aerospace	20,000	50	78,000
Kodak	20,000	50	82,000
Pacific Bell	18,000	50	65,000
Control Data	10,000	50	25,000
General Dynamics	6,500	100	95,000
Federal Express	6,500	90	20,000

Moreover, the executive may find a void between needs and desires. Communication by computer may be more rapid, accurate, and flexible than conversation between two individuals, but the social structure of an organization may demand the ability to link persons, groups, or remote locations. The executive appears to be leery of computer capability, based in part on the supposition that it may prove undependable. Another technological problem lies in the attitude of the executive. Most organizations, in the person of the CEO, tend to plan on today's needs rather than the needs of ten years from now. As a result most managers think of the future in terms of larger computers of the same type now available rather than looking at the innovations that may completely change the method of doing business in the future. Ten years ago the personal computer was just coming on the market, and the computer manufacturers were selling large mainframe units, yet today many of the personal computers have the power of the big machines of that day. Distributive networks of computers are being installed daily. Many workers are now working at home with computers linked to the office. The illustration is clear.

The wise manager will have an integrated approach to the social-technical system in which he/she works. Attention must be focused on the work processes as a whole rather than on any of the many parts, and the approach must be more complete than the usual managerial technique of the solution of immediate problems. The total system must be analyzed to define the purpose of the organization, to analyze the system as it exists and as it should be, to provide the specifications of new system design, and finally to implement the new system with the general concurrence of the work force. The technology, the people to use it, the structure of the organization, and the tasks to be performed should be integrated into a single performance unit.

THE EXECUTIVE AND THE MICROCOMPUTER

The business executive has been confronted with computers for a long time. The mainframe large-number crunchers have been with us for years and most executives have relied upon programmers and computer operators to operate them. Now, however, microcomputers with the power of previous mainframe computers can be placed on the desk of every executive and the manager is faced with the problem of understanding the operation and perhaps manipulating the keys. The newer systems are inexpensive and user friendly. Programming knowledge is not required. In addition, the user realizes quickly that material needed to do the job is embedded in the files of the corporation and the computer can open those files, enabling decision making based on facts rather than intuition.

Executives are faced with a series of decision points that they previously relegated to the information systems chief. They must make decisions on how microcomputers are to interface with the mainframes, how security of data is to be preserved when everyone can access the information, how to describe and enlist talent in new positions requiring higher skills of clerks and white-collar workers, and how to handle the shift of power when everyone has access to data. Computers and information flow were previously restricted to a group of professionals. New organization and new controls are now required. A mistake can still be made with a computer as well as without it, but the mistake may now be at a much lower level in the organization and be much harder to detect.

The problems must be faced *now*. There are some 900,000 computers in American business, almost all of them under personal control, and the number increases daily. Some companies are aware of the potential. United Technologies Corporation in 1982 launched a program for all senior executives, teaching them to use spread sheets, word processing, and communication with computers. Although this program is short and intense it shows that the day of the personal computer is here for the executive and will certainly spread. It will spread because the advantages of rapid communication, artificial intelligence operations, and the like cannot be turned over to a competitor.

But the provision of microcomputers on the desk top will not solve many inherent problems of the corporation. Productivity will not increase simply because computers are installed. In fact, computers may make the problems worse unless great care is taken. If documents are generated at the desk top how are they disseminated in the corporation? At what level should documents be generated? How is security preserved? How do we connect everyone in a proper sequence? Obviously, moving cards or discs around is no more satisfactory than moving paper. There is no central point of control. How can an organization be managed in this situation?

The executives facing the use of microcomputers in business must consider data management as a prime problem. With many different persons operating microcomputers the consistency of data, its format, and its compatibility with data from other machines must be carefully weighed. The use of different spread sheets, or different titles for subjects can lead to confusion and disarray.

This suggests that the new CEO must be willing to make a substantial investment in education of personnel. The end users must be trained not only to operate the machines, but in high-level skills in system operation. This is difficult when we realize that the end users are not really interested in the computer as such, but only as a means of advancing their ability to perform on the job. The result should be better decision making, not better computer operators.

However, the executive has overriding concerns. The old expression garbage in—garbage out (GIGO) becomes more of a problem when many individuals may be entering data and the control of quality is less certain. The control of access to data may be equally important. End user access to and ability to modify or maintain files independent of the corporation is a major problem. Finally, the computer may lead to waste of time and effort. End users may find it easier to solve problems with trial and error or use the computer as a calculator in place of reasoning. Nevertheless, computers are here to stay. The modern CEO will learn to live with them and use them for the advantage of his organization.

REFERENCES

1.   J. Weisner, "More R and D in the Right Places," *Issues in Science and Technology* 4 (1):13 (Fall 1987).

2.   "Responding to the Competitive Challenge: The Technological Dimension," *Bridge* 18 (1):3 (Spring 1988).

3.   R. M. Fulmer, *The New Management*. 4th ed. New York: Macmillan, 1987.

4.   A. Gabor, "What They Don't Teach You at Business School," *U.S. News and World Report*, July 13, 1987, p. 44.

5.   L. Thurow, *The Zero-Sum Society*. New York: Basic Books, 1980.

6.   S. Ikari, "The Japanese Work Ethic," *Sumitomo Magazine*, 1989, p. 23.

7.   D. Jarmul, "Will Cheaper Health Care Lead to Poorer Quality?" *National Research Council News Report* 37 (5):14 (May 1987).

8.   L. W. Sumney and R. M. Burger, "Revitalizing the U.S. Semiconductor Industry," *Issues in Science and Technology* 3 (4):32 (Summer 1987).

9.   A. Senia, "Companies Turn Old Ideas into Profits," *High Technology Business,* December 1987, p. 36.

10.   L. M. Branscomb, "National and Corporate Technology Strategies in an Interdependent World Economy," *Bridge* 16 (2):8 (Summer 1986).

11.   D. Greenberg, "Can Chicken-Coop Inventors Help Us Win?" *U.S. News and World Report,* July 27, 1987, p. 42.

12.   A. M. Squires, "Maestros of Technology," *Invention and Technology,* General Motors Corporation, Summer 1987, p. 24.

13.   "Ford Claims Honda Has Cost Advantage," *Houston Post,* August 24, 1987, p. 7F.

14.   K. Ibe, "The Illusion of Japan as Invincible Economic Giant," *Wall Street J.,* September 21, 1981, p. 35.

15.   W. G. Ouchi, *Theory Z.* New York: Avon, 1982.

16.   American Productivity and Quality Center, *Positioning Corporate Staff for the 1990's.* Houston, Tex.: American Productivity and Quality Center, 1988.

17.   K. D. Eason, "Patterns of Usage of a Flexible Information System." In *The Application of Information Technology,* edited by S. D. P. Harker and K. D. Eason. London: Taylor and Francis, 1990.

18.   T. K. Bikson and B. A. Gutek, *New Technology in the Office.* New York: Work in America Institute, 1980.

3
Organizing for Technical Development

We are beginning to see a combination of academia, industry, and government organized into a single entity to attack a particular problem. Such organizations are consortia. Consortia serve a research, teaching, advising, and informational function and thus are a part of educational and research institutions. It has not been so many years ago that the research consortium was confined to academic institutions or to groups in an industry.[1] The usual form was a group establishing common library facilities or interchanges. The HARLIC (Houston Area Research Library Consortium) is an example as is the cooperation between hospitals for joint laundry equipment use or purchase of supplies. Academic departments often collaborated with other departments in the same or another university and occasionally set up joint facilities such as research laboratories. The relationship between industry and the university was kept at arm's length. In fact, faculty members resented being labeled as practical and as doing industrial research. A few engineering schools maintained contact between the two alien camps. But the situation is rapidly changing.

We are now beginning to formulate a tighter definition of a consortium and to make legal restrictions upon it where consortia once were formal or informal depending on the arrangement between institutions. The definition is important. It should be emphasized that collaboration between individuals and/or departments and industry does not constitute a consortium and neither does the accumulation of industrial research in a research park. Consortia must be organized for a purpose. Most consortia have a general aim, such as development of a product from a basic research base.

The situation with regard to consortia is now changing. The faculty member eagerly seeks industrial contacts, patents are a significant source of income to universities, and industrial money is accepted as readily as federal grants. The organization of consortia among government, the universities, and industry is accepted as an every-day event. But these relationships create strains on the part of both industry and the university.

Strains within the university are evident at the administrative and faculty level. The administration is usually willing to accept funds for work to be conducted by a faculty member, but there are attendant problems. Some faculty members, in the fine arts for example, resent seeing an engineering professor with a fine income and other amenities as the result of some lucrative patent. The university may try to be even-handed, but it is difficult when one faculty member is bringing in large royalties to the university and another is costing university funds to support small projects. Universities are now required to be much more astute in negotiating rights to inventions, in making clear the responsibility and rewards to the faculty member who develops a new process, and in spelling out terms of agreements. Suits are being filed against universities on a regular basis by graduate students or fellows who may have participated in the research but gained inadequate financial rewards.

Industry on the other hand has problems in dealing with the university. The industry that wants to exploit an idea or invention from the university laboratory has a problem in securing rights involving several industries, each of which may lay claim to the same information. Industry may be asked to contribute to the support of a consortium and yet obtain no tangible results for some years as a result of the collaboration. When the bottom line is critical to the shareholder, the industry may press for more rapid solutions to its problems.

The difficult relationship has resulted in some universities refusing to accept large industrial connections and industry refusing to join a consortium for fear of losing proprietary interest. Nevertheless, the collaborative effort has grown by leaps and bounds and dozens of consortia are now organized for purposes ranging from information exchange to development of inventions. The venture capital companies are entering the field to establish individual research institutions such as the SRC (Semiconductor Research Corporation) organized by Billy Inman in Austin, Texas.

Consortia have problems related to university and industry attitudes. The faculty are often not interested in participating in consortia although their expertise may be essential. Multiple loyalties create problems. Many professors and some industries tend to say, "I can do it myself. Why should I share with others?" Many academic institutions fear the loss of autonomy especially if they are engaged in consortia with multimillion or billion dollar industries. Faculty members are unwilling to enter into a contract until funding is assured, while industry is unwilling to fund research until the services of experts are available. This chicken-and-egg problem may be insoluble in some cases. Many industries and some universities are also wary of government membership in a consortium. At one time, the major problem revolved around the open patent policy of the federal government but much of this problem has been partially resolved by new regulations. Faculty may not want to work on contracts involving defense or toxic materials. In addition, many institutions do not realize that the institution owes as much to the consortium as the consortium does to the institution.

The ways in which consortia organize are as varied as the institutions in which they are established. Some institutions such as MIT have elected to spin off small companies to exploit an idea and return a profit to the university which can amount to many millions of dollars per year. Other consortia have established nonprofit institutes in which industry, government, and academia collaborate, while others have maintained a direct university connection. The use of venture capital to spin off companies for development is rising steadily, while industry has also established separate facilities for consortia in some instances. Nevertheless, the problems are far outweighed by the advantage of consortium formation. Despite the problems of proprietary interest, companies have demonstrated great interest in joining groups interested in a single problem. The advantages are:

1. Drawing upon university basic science departments for ideas for future development.

2. Using research dollars more efficiently by pooling information.

3. Avoiding duplication of effort.

4. Undertaking large-scale expensive projects not easily handled alone.

5. Obtaining royalty-free patents from the consortium.

6. Learning about new disciplines impinging upon profits in the future.

7. Providing a source of employees from graduate students.

The university also gains benefits from the consortium through:

1. Ability to exploit the faculty member's idea.

2. Ability to obtain funds for support and development of the university.

3. Ability to attract new and perhaps expensive personnel.

4. Ability to obtain expensive equipment and space.

5. Ability to relate to the community and its development.

6. Ability to attract and pay graduate students.

7. Ability to obtain more and perhaps better publications.

The advantages are counterbalanced by some disadvantages. As an example, the Internal Revenue Service (IRS) has become interested in the consortium as a trust entity, such as the organization of semiconductor manufacturers into a single consortium to develop new devices. While it is true a consortium, especially if industry is heavily involved, may combine most of the total resources in a given field into a single monolithic structure (monopoly), this is not usually the case, and in fact, Congress has passed the National Cooperative Research Act to encourage joint efforts between industry and academia and between industries. However, the Justice Department and the Congress have not yet agreed.[2]

Disadvantages also lie closer to home. The university may find that a consortium will:

1. Divert loyalty from a school or department to the consortium.
2. Increase the demand on faculty for teaching and research.
3. Result in research-oriented faculty doing less teaching.
4. Result in conflict of interest, thus forcing graduate students into industrial research.
5. Create problems in promotion and tenure with staff who work in the consortium.

The industry may find that there are no exclusive rights to development of a device, support may be provided without visible immediate returns, and individual components of the consortium may be in competition to develop a product from a nonexclusive license.

A consortium is organized for many purposes. Although it is established with a major objective, the well-run group may perform many functions. As a general rule the consortium will:

1. Provide advice and information such as a library consortium.
2. Coordinate activities of a diverse group toward a common objective. MITI in Japan has performed this function admirably.
3. Facilitate activity toward a common goal. A group on solar energy development, semiconductor development, and the like, are examples.
4. Provide information. The Oak Ridge Institute for Nuclear Studies, a consortium of some fifty universities, serves largely as an information exchange on nuclear problems and possibilities.
5. Pursue development. This is probably the major thrust of consortia development.
6. Provide funds. The major thrust of the supercollider funding is the help provided to the economy of the state where it is to be located.
7. Provide direction. A consortium may pull together disparate research efforts into a common focus.

Regardless of the organization and the funding, a modern consortium should have a major goal in mind—the transfer of technology from a basic idea or principle into practical application. Technology transfer, to be discussed below, is critical to success with industry because unless there is a payoff in profit, most industries will not continue support for long periods of time.

Consortia usually have several organizational parameters present regardless of form. These include a focus of attack on a problem, possibilities for funding, ability to recruit personnel, a management structure, and formal agreements among all participants in the consortia. There must be a central point of command; governance by committee is useless. The consortium must work as an institution, not as the servant of an individual who may have conceived it. The consortium must satisfy mutual goals of all parties or it will not continue. The goals must be apparent and clearly stated and understood by every one. An administrative structure must be provided outside the structure of the university or the industry, or the project cannot succeed. The consortium must have a home, and agreements must spell out in detail how space and facilities will be provided.

Most consortia have an advisory board of representatives from all interested parties. Many groups have two advisory boards, one for technical input and one for university and industry representation. Most groups provide a specific path for technology innovation and transfer. This may include such items as publication rights (industry often wants publication delayed until exploitation is underway) and time before publication (usually thirty to sixty days), patent rights (industry may want exclusivity), and royalty payments, and these must be clearly spelled out in the agreement.

The infrastructure of a consortium may be highly variable. One customary procedure is to charge all industrial components an annual fee based on corporate sales. In return the consortium will provide access to expertise in the university faculty, publications, nonexclusive patents, seminars, graduate students for summer or other employment, annual meetings for dissemination of information, and services such as literature searches.

The interest of industry and often of the government for consortium formation is the innovation and technology transfer from the research laboratory to practical purposes. Industry, especially large industry, suffers from a lack of entrepreneurship, and for it to take a risk on new products requires an unacceptable risk of net worth. As a result the company often simply wishes to improve old products. This places industry at odds with academia. Industry is interested in rapid transfer of knowledge, exploitation, and return on investment while the university may be interested in full development of an idea. This is an increasingly critical situation when the Germans, the Italians, and especially the Japanese can develop products more quickly, produce them with greater efficiency, and at higher quality than American counterparts. At one time the United States was noted for the quantity and quality of its inventions. Now the Japanese and others are filing more patents and exploiting them more rapidly than the Americans.[3] Collaboration with research faculties is one way to reverse the process and the consortium may be the answer. However, many high technology enterprises in the university never get off the ground because they cannot mix technology with good business sense. Collaboration with industry may be the answer.

Consortia organized with government agencies may not be the perfect solution. Work is done on contract with requests for proposal (RFPs) that are very specific and do not allow deviation in research directions. However, it is possible to consider the organization of consortia involving all three elements.

There are four qualities to be determined in organizing a consortia for technological transfer. They are the quality of the management team, the availability of funds, the quality of the technology, and the image of success displayed by the consortium. Obviously the most important element in the beginning is the technology. Researchers believe their invention will revolutionize an area of science but all too often the better mousetrap only traps the consortium. Thus, determination of a fair market value is critical to success. Technology can get high marks only if it has the potential to create new products that can be patented and protected, and have a high market potential. The availability of funds is critical and this depends in part upon the image. A consortium headed by a Nobel prize winner is more likely to be listened to when a new invention is discussed. Management is important. Every element concerned must have confidence in the management and its ability to put together facilities, ideas, personnel, and money to create a viable product. Choice of a director becomes a major task of any consortium. Then all elements must work closely together for success to be obtained.

If a research consortium is a success, the output will be a salable product. Exploitation then becomes a major concern. There are several established methods. The MIT method is to spin off a small company producing a product, making a profit, using the faculty as management and technical staff, and returning a percentage of the profits to the institution. MIT has been phenomenally successful in this type of operation. Many universities would not be happy with faculty engaged in employment outside the university or with teaching and research time diluted by management requirements. In other cases, the university has set up an institute or similar organization within a department or the university to exploit the ideas. Industry may contract with the institution for total research effort or a share of output of research and the institute is free to seek government contracts or grants. A separate freestanding organization set up as a nonprofit corporation can receive grants and contracts, license industry, and conduct research and development. This organization may bleed faculty members from the university as consultants or researchers. Industry may elect to be the source of support, as with SRC, mentioned above, and provide facilities, employ faculty on a parttime basis, and direct the research toward industry goals. Each organization may be composed of a full-time staff with part-time input from the elements of the consortium. Examples of each kind of organization can be found in one consortium or another.

A new type of consortium is beginning to develop as the individual states realize that development of industry and therefore state development depends upon a research base. Virginia, for example, has set up the Center for Innovative Technology (CIT), making grants to university researchers, and focusing on technology development and patenting with transfer and commercialization of products that appear to be feasible. The cooperation with industry is stressed. Virginia, through the CIT, has elected to develop specific areas where major expertise exists in the universities. In four years CIT has involved more than 200 industries in 300 projects in some 20 or more institutions.

Texas has developed an Applied Technology Initiative from which large grants are made to potentially commercially feasible projects in universities. The universities are expected to exploit the ideas as they develop. Other states have plans serving the same purpose but varying in design.

The research consortium is an entity whose time has come. There are now fifty or more industrial consortia and dozens of university-based or supervised organizations. All are concentrated on the technology transfer of ideas developed in basic research and all encompass academia and industry with the government playing an increasing role as the regulations governing patent protection of federally supported projects loosen. Hopefully, such arrangements will again permit America to take the lead in world markets and technical development.

There are now some 2,900 industrial organizations affiliated with many universities, but 40 universities lead the way with MIT having 275 such arrangements. More than 500 foreign industries are involved. The total investment is about $2 billion per year. The academic-industrial consortium is here to stay.[1]

It may be worth mentioning there are many other forms of inter-organizational arrangements. Some, like MIT, spin off their own corporations from the university research and may have university funds (in the form of a research foundation) to fund startup costs.

Other groups have been able to find venture capital and begin with total control of profits and production. As a result there is an increasing technology base founded in R and D and developed into products by a industry. Technology not only affects the product, it also affects the workplace, the employees, and the managers in the way communications are handled, data is managed, and work is accomplished.[4] The consortium is the ideal solution.

THE JOINT VENTURE

A form of consortium is developing in the world trade centers. Companies are entering into agreements to join forces to create a product using the best features of each company. We have remarked on the agreements to produce cars jointly for the American market between Japanese and American and European auto makers but with the standards of quality demanded by foreign manufacturers. Such joint ventures spread the risk of failure, achieve economy of scale, combine patents, and may avoid restrictive tariffs or legislation.

Cities and states, as well as two or more industrial enterprises, have entered into joint agreements. Cities see financial returns in employment, tax bases, and other more intangible assets and have aggressively sought ventures with foreign manufacturers. Some forty states and dozens of cities have trade representatives in Japan and Europe. The agreement usually requires the political entity to furnish roads, electricity, and other infrastructure, and in some cases to provide plants for lease or the land upon which to build them. Intercession is often required with local unions, and additional schools and other amenities must be arranged.

Such joint ventures are both an advantage and a disadvantage to the community. The city, for example, sees a larger tax base, more employment, and an enhanced reputation, but there may also be tax concessions to the new company that may erode the tax base, priorities may become mixed as politicians see the political advantage of large scale industrial clout, and other community improvements may be sacrificed to provide new roads and schools for industrial growth.

Innovation is the output of the consortium. However, for innovation to be successful we must carefully distinguish between the new versus a modification of an old process, radical changes versus incremental changes, and science versus engineering.[5] American managers have been deficient in all of these. The quick fix rather than the new idea has been the method adopted by American manufacturers in designing automobile engines. Other countries have proceeded to innovate with rotary engines. The Z-idea of corporation management originated in the United States, was exploited by the Japanese and is now being reimported as a completely new idea. We must reexamine our approach to innovation and technology.

REFERENCES

1.   D. C. Neal, ed., *Consortia and Interinstitutional Cooperation.* London: Collier Macmillan, 1988.

2.   H. Visser and E. Schoorl, *Trade in Transit.* Boston: Kluwer Academic Publishers, 1987.

3.   S. Ramo, *The Business of Science.* New York: Hill and Wang, 1988.

4.   *R and D. Productivity.* Culver City, Calif.: Hughes Aircraft, 1974.

5.   Z. Griliches, "R and D and Productivity," *Science* 237:31 (1987).

4

Educating for International Business

A typical scenario of American industry goes as follows. The American auto industry is producing large, expensive, gas-guzzling cars. A competitor arises in Japan producing small, well-made, gas-saving vehicles. In a matter of a few years the American manufacturers' share of the auto market falls from 50 percent to about 35 percent. The profit margin drops drastically. The drop of a few percentage points represents billions of dollars of income and profit. What is the solution? Obviously the best answer is competition. And how does one compete? Should the American solution be to learn to build excellent cars using Yankee ingenuity and a productive work force? The American answer has not been initiative and better know-how. It is to put pressure on Congress to raise taxes on foreign imports to restore the level playing field, or rather to tilt it in the opposite direction, toward the Americans. Of course, raising import duties raises prices, raises taxes, deprives the customer of bargains in cars, and increases inflation. But this does not prevent the automobile company from making a profit and paying its executives a high salary for such an innovative approach. They have taken the risk of overall damage to the economy to protect a dividend rather than educating the executive to the new directions. Lester Thurow has driven one more nail into the coffin of American industry by his comments. He points out that the innovative Americans have led the world in five of nine major technology innovations and have placed second in the other four, but Americans are slow to adopt the changes through engineering and to place them on an assembly line. Thus Americans lag behind several other countries in development of the ideas to practical use. Also, the United States spends about 3 percent of sales on quality control while the Germans, as one example, spend more than 10 percent. Thurow's comment is borne out by a survey of CEOs who thought the road to the top executive positions led through financial dealing (35 percent) as compared to manufacturing (5 percent). This may well explain why innovation in manufacturing does not come from within a company. [1] The results are obvious.

Exports of high technology products have dropped more than 30 percent in ten years. We must realize that we are now a global economy. This is clearly demonstrated by several facts.

1. We owe a tremendous debt to other countries and the service costs are high.

2. The sources of supply are global. Companies are resorting to overseas labor and materials.

3. Money flows globally. We now trade twenty times as much in money as we do in goods.

4. The United States has lost the dominant position in world markets.

5. Political factors cause levy of high tariffs as a result of pressure by partisan groups.

DEALING WITH THE WORLD

The relative decrease in productivity in the United States is due in large part to increasing wages and benefits and to the shift from a production to a service economy. Poor management practices contribute greatly to the problem. And poor management results from poor training and education. The result is loss, not only in the country, but in foreign markets where we have been unable to compete with other countries.

A host of products can be purchased more cheaply and in better quality abroad than in the United States.[2] Foreign innovations in such areas as steel making have made serious inroads into exports. Yet we must have foreign markets—the United States cannot become an insular power.[3] So American industry is turning its attention to technology transfer, particularly to the lesser developed countries (LDC) in an attempt to invade foreign markets once again. Several companies such as CocaCola, Xerox, Kodak, and others have made serious gains in foreign markets by applying a few general rules. They have learned the lesson of producing high-quality, low-cost goods. They wait patiently for a market to develop, often only after many years, they adjust practice to local conditions, and they use local customs and employees. Finally they build on already developed strengths.

American business must learn many lessons in investing in foreign areas. The transfer of technology is not an American forte, but must be exploited to the maximum.

The ability to transfer technology, to invest in plant capacity, and to develop the technology to suit a new situation is crucial and has not been done well in many cases. Transfer of high technology has been attempted in countries where financial and other infrastructure was not present, where educational levels were insufficient to support technology, where training facilities were not available. Proper education of our citizens would provide the information about a country, its mores, and its ability to accept innovation.

We tend to forget that developed countries have several advantages the LDCs do not. We have a developed infrastructure providing communications and transportation as well as other advantages and a knowledge base in relatively well-educated citizens that can be tapped for development. We have developed automated techniques and the use of computers not available in LDCs and we have less need for raw materials to process salable goods. The facts point out a clear line of development for the LDCs. They must rely for the foreseeable future upon human-power and the things that can be produced with the use of large and untrained human resources. Any attempt to replace labor with technology will result in chaos and massive unemployment and unrest.

American companies have a tendency to create wholly owned subsidiaries in foreign countries. This creates problems with management and with local resistance. Japan, on the other hand, has usually worked closely with the local population in collaborative arrangements. The companies from the United States also tend to create large complex organizations while the Japanese have created many small companies that are more closely integrated. Technology has not been licensed by American companies other than to owned companies and independent licensing is not looked upon with favor. Other countries have been much freer in this regard. We tend to establish companies in foreign countries that are heavily slanted toward the provision of services and consumer goods while other countries invest much more heavily in companies using local talent in manufacturing. The American manager typically stays one, two, or perhaps three years, and is rotated home before learning the customs of the country and the ways of doing business there. Other developed countries require their expatriates to make a long-term commitment of many years.

The importance of the international market cannot be overemphasized and as a result all developed countries are in direct competition. It has become apparent that some attempt must be made to develop countries so that they can receive and successfully apply technology. Two methods of attack have been used.

The United States has typically relied upon nonprofit organizations to develop a country to the point where it can apply technology supplied by industry. The development has been oriented toward the infrastructure and the general level of education and appreciation of technology. The Agency for International Development (AID), the Rockefeller Foundation, and others have provided educational opportunities, developed water and food supplies, and designed transportation systems. Volunteers in Technical Assistance (VITA), International Executive Services Corps (IESC), and Fund for Multinational Management Education (FMME) have been aimed at more specific national expertise. A computerized list of over 60,000 technical reports assists countries in developing a structure for technical development. On the other hand, many countries and their companies, Japan for example, rely upon the individual company or a large trading company rather than private nonprofit organizations or the government to the input for development.

ENTERING FOREIGN MARKETS

An organization entering into a foreign market must understand that many objectives must be accomplished in short order. Managers must be trained, technical
personnel must be updated, employees must be hired and trained, customers and
distributors must be trained, training facilities must be established and staffed,
fellowships must usually be established to train future managers, and home office personnel must be trained and on the job.[4]

Many American companies wish to transfer the technology per se as an end
result whereas the end result for most recipients is economic growth. The technology is only a way to achieve it. Because of this misunderstanding, many
companies have the tendency to institute a technology the country cannot absorb
either in terms of size and complexity or of operating skills of the employees. In
the past, enormous dams, steel plants, and other showpieces have been built
when the technological development was not sufficient to operate them. One of
us once served as an advisor to an African country regarding the need for health
care. After a survey of a country of many millions with the number of competent
physicians counted in the tens, it was recommended that physician assistants be
trained and located in the bush to treat the local populations. We were told,
"That's not what we want. We want a hospital that can do open heart surgery."
This clearly indicates the difference between expectation and ability that many
companies must face when doing business in LDCs.

The choice of location is critical. In Thailand, with a large population of
well-educated, college-trained individuals, many of whom are looking for work,
the development of technology is much quicker and easier than in Indonesia
where the population is largely uneducated and untrained except in agricultural
pursuits. The existing infrastructure is parallel with the educational structure as
one might expect.

The choice of technology is also critical. Thailand, with a rapidly expanding
population and a decreasing land area for food production, badly needs fertilizer
production, improved genetics for agricultural crops, crop storage methods, farm
machinery, and new agricultural products, while Bali and Java in Indonesia, with
adequate agricultural area for the population, need infrastructure to develop industry for large cities and other sources of off-the-farm income. We must understand
that technology is not only machines and tools but is also the infrastructure,
people, and organization. In addition, Americans have not yet learned the lesson
taught many years ago by E. Schumacher in his book *Small Is Beautiful*, that
improvement in technology is a series of slow, short steps rather than a gigantic
leap.

It has been suggested that the Third World suffers from disabilities that will
create problems. Automation in most developing countries cannot be devel-

oped with an uneducated work force and a lack of technical support. The developing countries lack the knowledge to develop a technical base. The infrastructure
that is basic to transportation and communication allowing for technical development does not exist. Finally, as technology develops, there is decreased need for raw materials, the lifeblood of most underdeveloped countries.
When these almost insurmountable obstacles are combined with the need to keep
a very large and under-educated work force employed, the need for technology
can be questioned. In addition, these facts lead to the conclusion that the Third
World will not become a ready competitor in the near term. However, we must
keep in mind the rapid growth of Korea and Japan.

Stewart and Nihei [4] have summed up the process by listing some of the requirements for successful technology transfer as development of scaled-down
technology, reduction in the number of product options chosen, lower performance standards, use of local materials, inexpensive packaging, increased investment in exportable products, technical support to local firms, better use of time
and skills of expatriates, and rapid turnover of trained employees to domestic
economy.

In a time of rising international competition, the manager must be prepared
to deal on the international market with well-versed competitors who are better
trained to handle the problems. We can sum up the excuses for American failures in the marketplace by using a few examples from often repeated clichés:

1. They will have to slow down soon, then we will catch up.
Unfortunately, productivity is higher elsewhere.

2. Products occur in cycles and we are at the end of one and have
not yet begun the next. If this is true why are 100 percent of VCRs, invented in the United States, made in foreign plants mostly for American
markets?

3. Service represents the next industrial revolution and the United
States leads the world in service industry. But service produces nothing
salable and moving a worker into service decreases productivity by 39
percent.[3]

The health care industry with little improvement in mortality rates to show
for rapidly expanding costs is an excellent example. So are the lawyers and accountants who contribute nothing to the productivity. Automation that actually
may increase the clerical work force rather than decreasing it is another example.

An examination of the problems listed above suggests that changes will
occur only if the American white-collar worker is willing to change. There is little sign this is occurring.

America must look to its laurels on another front as well. We have tried
rather unsuccessfully in competition with the Far East and Europe to take world
markets in the LDCs. The tables are now turned. We are seeing foreign funds
used not only to provide competition in goods here at home but also to dominate

our industrial complex. Last year some nineteen companies with more than $1 billion capital each, became multinational.[1] Foreign investors have supplied more than 3 million jobs in the United States, and have increased productivity 10 percent in those companies they have taken over.

However, this results in a final flight of capital as profits are siphoned off to the foreign country or the parent corporation. The United States must change its stance in order to compete, especially within the next few years when the European Economic Community (EEC) drops all trade and monetary barriers and we will be facing larger and equally developed nation(s).

REFERENCES

1.   G. Packard, "Partners in Prosperity," *Atlantic Monthly,* September 1988, p. 41.

2.   U. C. Lehner, "Aid to Japan's Growth," *Wall Street J.,* September 14, 1981, p. 1.

3.   M. W. Karmin et al., "Will the U.S. Stay Number One?" *U.S. News and World Report,* February 2, 1987, p. 18.

4.   C. T. Stewart, Jr. and Y. Nihei, *Technology Transfer and Human Factors.* Lexington, Mass.: Lexington Books, 1987.

5.   E. F. Schumacher, *Small Is Beautiful.* New York: Harper and Row, 1973.

5

The Japanese Puzzle

The Japanese and their style of business have been mentioned several times thus far.[1] There is a reason. Their educational system is based on the needs of the country, and the students are oriented toward technology and productivity from an early age. The Japanese children are perhaps three grades or more ahead of their American counterparts and their knowledge is much greater in science, suggesting that Japan may well overtake the United States in new product development in the near future. For these and other reasons American executives fear the Japanese more than any other competition, with some justification. If we do not change our ways, we are likely to be unable to compete in the 2000s. The Japanese school system may train by rote, which is the antithesis of the American method, but the students do come out with knowledge and the ability to fit into the social system, while in America they do not. Furthermore, the Japanese style of business is the direct opposite of the American way.

With a tremendous trade surplus the Japanese are investing heavily in American enterprise and their influence is felt in every corner of business. This sends shivers of dread through the business community. Finally, the American business person does not fear the English or the German invasions (also very large) as much as the Japanese. The standard of living is increasing rapidly in Japan (almost $20,000 per person last year), exceeds that of the United States, and the annual growth rate of the economy is greater. There should be cause for alarm.

Yet all is not rosy in Japan.[2] Problems of competition within the country raise real questions of survival for some companies.[3] The balance of trade places pressure on businesses that export heavily. The Japanese stock market is outgaining the American market, and this may lead to inflation. The homogeneity of the Japanese industry tends to breed careful agreement and avoidance of any eccentricity or straying from the norm. The rigidity of the industrial enterprise is evident. Finally, the Japanese require a labor-intensive product in order to maintain near total employment in a more socialistic society.

Japanese industry fails in several conspicuous ways. The concept of lifetime employment, while a great social stride, suffers from several faults. In a declining economy (Japan has yet to face this, although as we write there have been dramatic changes in the stock market) lifetime employment could be a drag on the economy.

Second, the lifetime employment concept applies to only some of the work force. Farmers, small businesses, and others do not observe the practice, which is confined largely to the big companies. The Japanese also have established an early retirement system (in the fifties) in order to support a growing work force and this creates major social problems. The retiree often does not have a living stipend and must take another position. Such positions are hard to obtain because of the company loyalty inspired by the lifetime employment concept. Any new employee must start at the bottom and work his way upward again. Finally, there is a large force, mainly women, called temporary employees, who receive none of the benefits, are paid a low wage, and are outside the retirement system.

On the other hand, the Japanese economy is adjusted to the needs of the country. Taxes are low and a very high savings rate by the population as a whole (some four to five times the American rate) accumulates capital for investment. The educational system is designed to turn out the kind of graduates that industry needs. The Japanese are willing to plan for a long-term return on investment.

All of these qualities point to some reasons for Japanese success. But as K. Ibe has pointed out, many problems lie beneath the surface.[4]   The small company faces intense internal competition. The basic industries such as agriculture have not been highly mechanized and have low productivity. The rate of return on investment in Japanese industry as a whole is probably about one-half that of the United States. In addition, Japan must import large quantities of energy, food, and raw materials in order to survive.

Despite the shortcomings, the Japanese have virtues that could well be emulated by most nations. We could well consider employing some Japanese attributes in our production system. The work ethic is foremost. Americans have been proud of the Puritan work ethic of the Northeast United States, but the Japanese really work.[5] The average Japanese puts in about 2,150 hours per year as compared to the American 1,900, the French 1,650, and the West German 1,610 hours. That labor is a virtue has long been an ethic in Japanese schools and society. The tradition is a long one, Confucius advocated the work ethic, and it was strengthened by the Meiji period when Japan was first modernized. One has only to consider the school system. The typical Japanese child goes to school five and one-half days a week almost all year, does three hours of homework a night in order to compete, and usually employs special tutors at night and on weekends if college entrance exams are to be passed. Teachers have no disciplinary problems and are highly respected. Contrast this with the American system. The college system admits only the brightest students determined by a series of tests at various levels. The elitist system is a far cry from the United States where everyone who can finish high school can go to college. Yet, about one-third of Japanese children go to college, and most finish, compared to a much poorer rate in the United States.

In addition, the Japanese approaches work differently from his American counterpart. As Edward Hall has pointed out so effectively, people can be divided into two classes, monochromatic and polychronatic.[6] The monochromatic person tends to do one job at a time, makes strict time commitments, and does not think in context. This person must have large amounts of information to perform a job, will closely adhere to plans, is concerned about privacy of others, shows great respect for private property, and emphasizes short-term relationships and promptness. This leads to an assembly-line intellect with individuals concentrating only on one part of one job.

The polychronatic person, on the other hand, does many things at once, is subject to rapid change, works by context rather than information because the information has already been gathered, is committed to personal relationships rather than privacy, and builds long-term relationships. The Americans as a whole are monochromatic while the Japanese are polychronatic and this automatically creates a source of conflict in the approach to business by the two societies.

This difference in attitude creates conflicts between the two cultures, especially when business is under discussion. Some examples may illustrate the problem. The privacy ethic in our culture leads to the "twentieth floor" syndrome of private offices, small-group discussions, and adherence to schedules. The Japanese, on the other hand (together with Latins and Arabs), live in an open society with large offices, require long periods of time to make arrangements and to establish personal contacts, are less concerned with agenda and precise time schedules. The American is committed to short-term precise schedules while the polychronatic individual is oriented to the long term.

This leads to direct conflict. The American wants an immediate answer to a problem with a precise time schedule for resolution, while other societies are content with long-term solutions and thus are willing to take time to make decisions and implement them. We can compete with this difference in attitude, but to do so we must approach education in a different manner. The core curriculum as proposed by several studies may be a partial answer.

The lifestyle of the two countries leads to contrasts in definitions of excellence. The ability of Japanese management to handle the work force is in direct contrast to the United States. During the '50's and '60's Japan had great strikes and confrontations. The labor movement almost became Communist, but did not. The realization of Japanese labor power came to the managers and they took steps to insure the cooperation of the labor force with management. The system developed worked so well that a strike is now likely to last only a few hours simply to demonstrate some worker dissatisfactions and it is unlikely to disrupt an industry, in contrast to the massive strikes in steel, automobiles, and other areas in the United States where management has not learned to work with the labor force. Labor-management relations in Japan are no longer confrontational because each has a stake in the future of the industry, while in America the worker has an interest only in his salary.

Some attempts are being made to carry the system over to the United States. In Batavia, Ohio, the Ford plant has adopted Japanese principles of employment and production. A complete shift of understanding was necessary. In Japan the workers are assumed to perform independently on the job while in the United States they are presumed to need intensive supervision to work. Therefore, as Japanese plants were established in America, the work attitude had to change. A typical example is an automobile assembly plant formed in cooperation between Japanese and American car manufacturers.[7] The plant was built with the Japanese worker in mind. It is designed to expand by 30 percent in the next three years without adding a single worker. The whole American concept of productivity had to be altered. The changes resulted in greater output, more satisfaction on the part of workers, and a better product. Excellence as a Japanese hallmark was carried over to the American worker, albeit with considerable trauma to some employees. The United Automobile Workers (UAW) opposed the changes, but the workers accepted them.

Hopefully the Japanese may teach us something. "Made in America" was once a label commanding respect around the world. Now it is a slogan indicating goods to be shunned in many quarters. Lee Iacocca has appeared on television complaining that when American and Japanese brand name cars are made in the same factory, the public prefers the Japanese models. The average American car requires about three repairs to one for the Japanese makes, Iacocca notwithstanding.

We have mentioned that 70 percent of the delicate components of IBM computers are made in Japan because of these problems. All VCRs are made in Asia although they were invented in the United States. Today not a single U.S. company produces home VCRs although they are ubiquitous in our population.

The Japanese have been derided in the past as copiers of the technology of others, but this is no longer true. The Japanese take out many more patents than the United States and take out more patents *in* the United States, suggesting we have lost the technological edge. And the mark of excellence in technology is innovation as revealed by patents.[3]

The fault lies with the American managers who have not demanded quality and innovation as a part of original production. And a large part of the fault lies in the failure to insist on an educational standard that would make the American worker competitive. We do not have an excellent education system and therefore do not teach excellence in the classroom.

Defective parts, outmoded assembly techniques, and other production defects add up to 20 percent to the price of American products. There is little wonder that we cannot compete. Step-by-step production of items with each part of the assembly as a separate unit finally melded together has vastly increased costs.

American car makers have been satisfied with marginal quality in order to improve the bottom line, and events prove this no longer pays. The one glimmer of light is Ford's new group production-line method that has improved Ford quality remarkably in a short time.

Industrial robots were invented in the United States but 60 percent of all robots installed in U. S. plants last year came from Japan, and at last count Japan had about 67,000 robots on assembly lines compared to 14,000 in the United States. The loss of the semiconductor market is another example of the failure of managers to use talent to the best advantage.[7]

The shortsightedness of the Americans in assuming that other countries could not equal the United States in productivity are cases in point. Japan has until now been the best example, but Korea, Taiwan, Italy, Germany, and England are all vying for American markets with better products. In retaliation the Americans chose the shortsighted approach, they invested in cheap labor markets overseas. This effort reduced the cost of products, but it left American plants to become more and more outdated and inefficient. The Japanese in particular have beaten us at our own game. They have moved plants to the United States, hired American workers, and, using Japanese management, have outcompeted American manufacturers and sent the money home. As one example of Japanese efficiency, when Toyota took over a plant formerly run by General Motors, they cut job classifications from 80 to 4 and the time of assembly from 36 to 17 hours and produced a better quality car.

Education is again at fault. As we shall stress again, the Japanese train CEOs as technical workers with a complete background in all aspects of the industry. America trains its CEOs as business people often with little or no knowledge of the processes they control.

Unfortunately, the Japanese system has a major defect. In many of the very large companies, the enterprise is family-owned, and the relatives are groomed for high company positions. Sumitomo, for example, is proud of the 400-year-old tradition of continuous management in the same family.[3],[8] The Japanese company, therefore suffers from a long-embedded bureaucracy. However, in one respect, the concept is good. There is long-term continuity and the long-range objectives of the organization can be carried out by the trained successors, while in the United States, a change in CEO may mean a total change in the company directions.

There are other areas for discussion. The Japanese farmer is engaged in a highly intensive operation, farming small plots of land, raising as many crops per year as possible, and demanding support from the government. In this respect, the Japanese farmer outdoes his American counterpart. The cost of rice in Japan is perhaps ten times the world market price, as the Japanese government supports the farmer and prohibits imports.[9]

This discussion leads to a definition of excellence. Excellence is determined by the decision to accomplish a given task in the best possible way and at the lowest cost consistent with quality. This requires long-range planing, stated objectives, and cooperation between all elements of the plan. This is as true in planning a new automobile assembly line and the kind of car to be produced as it is in determining the kind of education our children should receive for the future employment market, or the decision to be made between cost and benefit in a health care system relying upon technology to improve care. And the United States is lagging behind in these areas. We have not determined the most desirable kind of education and insisted upon quality to achieve it. We have not determined the kind of health care we want (prevention vs. treatment) and how to achieve it, and we have not been able to bite the bullet for good government and thus eliminate the sleaze factor. Until we can accomplish some of these aims, we will not have excellence in the United States. The Japanese standards of excellence are higher than ours and will remain so unless we make a conscious effort to change the situation.

The only hope is a change in the educational system. We must begin to educate youngsters toward a work ethic and the need for knowledge, to educate the managers toward a greater understanding of the products they make, and to educate the worker to a greater cooperation with his fellows. Koji Matasomoto pointed out that the reason for success of the Japanese system is education. Education of the worker to encourage development along with continuing education of the manager to work with employees; education of junior and senior employees to learn from each other; education of the worker to be his own quality control system and the supervisor of the production process; and development of a system of suggestion implementation for rapid innovation. We would do well to heed the advice.

REFERENCES

1. M. F. Deutsch, *Doing Business with the Japanese*. New York: New American Library, 1983.

2. M. J. Wolf, *The Japanese Conspiracy*. New York: Empire Books, 1983.

3. K. Ohmae, "Japan vs. Japan: Only the Strong Survive," *Wall Street J.*, January 26, 1981, p. 20.

4. K. Ibe, "The Illusion of Japan as Invincible Economic Giant," *Wall Street J.*, September 21, 1981, p. 35.

5. S. Ikari, "The Japanese Work Ethic," *Sumitomo Corporation Bulletin*, Summer 1987.

6. E. T. Hall and M. R. Hall, *Hidden Differences*. Garden City, N.Y.: Anchor Press/Doubleday, 1987.

7. R. T. Pascale and A. G. Athos, *The Art of Japanese Management*. New York: Simon and Schuster, 1981.

8. D. Greenberg, "Can Chicken-Coop Inventors Help Us Win?" *U.S. News and World Report*, July 27, 1987, p. 42.

9. I. Shapiro, "Second Thoughts about Japan," *Wall Street J.*, June 5, 1981, p. 24.

6

Education for the Workplace

America's shame is its schools. We have no commitment to learning, no evidence that a student is taught to his potential, and every indication that the system is failing day by day. We are in competition with the Japanese and the Europeans who consider education to be essential and insist upon quality and quantity. The Japanese believe in education from the cradle to the grave. A few examples illustrate the differences. We have been more concerned with discrimination and education of the less talented than training the leaders of the next generation. Our Scholastic Aptitude Test (SAT) scores trend generally downward and some 20 percent of all Americans cannot function in a literate society and probably twice that number cannot function in a technological society. Dropout rates average about 30 percent for whites, 40 percent for Latin-Americans, 50 percent for blacks, and perhaps 10 percent for Asian students. Surveys conducted by the school systems and by the Gallup poll for the National Geographic Society suggest that a large percent of Americans are illiterate when asked about geography, politics, and current affairs. School in the United States rarely exceeds 5 days a week with many holidays—180 days and 36 weeks per year and the average student does about 30 minutes of homework per day. The typical Japanese student goes to school five and one-half days per week, 240 days per year in 44 weeks and does about three hours of homework per day. [1]

In addition, any Japanese student with ambition toward college usually spends an additional two to four hours per day in study, often with a special tutor. Moreover, the Japanese students are forced into a rigid curriculum of mathematics, physics, and other sciences.They are in a classroom with fifty other students at all times, and perform their own janitorial services. American students do little except for extracurricular activity. American educators are aghast if more than twenty-five students are in a classroom, and the American student is left with a choice of electives permitting an easy course and sure graduation. Promotion is often based on "keeping up with the fellows" rather than accomplishment, and there has been a spate of stories about athletes who graduate without being able to read or write. Of even greater importance, the Japanese student is socialized, learning cooperation, work habits, and attention to detail to make him a good employee.

To illustrate the problem, let us summarize the results of a National Geographic survey. Americans rank low in geographic knowledge and last in the eighteen-to-twenty-four-year-old age group of any developed nation. American students were unable to identify 50 percent of all landmarks as compared to Swedish students who identified 90 percent. Despite the fact we have fought a war and stationed troops in the Persian Gulf, 75 percent of all American students could not find the gulf on a map. A similar percentage did not know where Vietnam was located. About one-half of the students were not able to find Japan or France on a map. Of greater concern is the fact that younger students do worse than older students on these questions, indicating that our system is deteriorating rather than improving. Also of great concern are adult Americans who have been trained in our school system but do not know where the apartheid policy is in effect, which countries have nuclear weapons, or the location of the recent conflict in Central America.

The education accorded to youngsters does not correlate well with the money spent to develop the school systems. Texas does not rank high on the academic totem pole and it spends about $4,000 per pupil per year in grades K-12. One would assume that $4,000 would buy a good education. However, it turns out the highest ranking school scholastically, as determined by the standardized tests, receives about 35 percent less per pupil than the school receiving the highest amount per pupil ($4,800), which ranks twelfth. Furthermore the top scholastic ranked school has an average SAT score of 950 compared to the school spending the most money per pupil, with a SAT of about 900. Money does not necessarily secure a good education. It is certainly true that if the amount of money spent per pupil decreases below a maintenance level, then scores do correlate with available funds.

Money, the financial magazine, in May 1990 looked at two schools in Illinois and New Jersey with the same enrollment, dollars spent per pupil, resources, and family income. They found that one school sent a large proportion of its students to college and had high SAT scores while the other had many fewer college attendees, low scores, and other problems. [2] Obviously family income and expenditure per pupil were not the deciding factors. We must examine this type of data to determine what is wrong with our schools.

The abysmal results of our educational system are reflected in the work force. New technology like computers and robots demand a higher level of education to operate and maintain. And there is no question but that there is a decrease in quality of the work force. Baily has suggested this may be due in part to the decrease in quality of education caused by a lack of mathematical and language skills in the younger worker. [3]

Much of the problem has been blamed on the family. The American family is concerned with divorce, abortion, and day care while families of many other countries are concerned largely with the children and their development. The extremely high rate of teenage unmarried pregnancies (by far the largest in the world) contributes to the decline of scholastic ambition.

We can return here to a point that has been made before. American managers have consistently failed to seek cooperation of workers, to encourage learning and productivity, and to train workers properly.[4]   When the Government Accounting Office (GAO) studied two plants in close proximity that produced coal using the same techniques and procedures, it found one produced 58 tons per worker per day while the other produced 242 tons per day. The only measurable difference was the cooperation between management and the workers and the kind of training, suggesting that improvement can also be made in this area.

We are in a deep slough of trouble in the United States. Although the United States still receives its share of Nobel prizes, demonstrating the presence of outstanding innovation, the waters are getting deeper and darker with regard to development. The gap between innovation and production is widening.

We are not training the people we need to keep the processes of society active. A large part of the problem is that other workers of the world are passing us by enforcing higher standards of education from kindergarten onward. A recent article in *Science* pointed out that we are attracting fewer and fewer of the brighter students into science; more than 50 percent of doctorate degrees, especially in engineering, are awarded to foreign students; United States student enrollment in the sciences rose by 1 percent in the last ten years while foreign enrollment rose 23 percent in the same period; and the United States share in technical literature publication dropped by about 20 percent during the same period.[5]

All of these symptoms are aggravated by the shift to military R and D in terms of both employment and funding. The high employment by industry of the holders of baccalaureate degrees in engineering has discouraged commitments to advanced degrees and has exacerbated the situation.

The solution lies largely within academia. We must be able to provide good teachers, to attract students to graduate work, and to provide the facilities needed. The solution for many problems in industry lies in education and the understanding that much of education in the future will be science oriented. Industry must help prepare workers for the change.

Of course, much depends upon the teacher. Teaching was at one time considered to be an honorable profession. Today, in the United States, it is not. Paper work, unruly pupils, and low salaries have driven the teachers from the classroom. Experience of the large universities has clearly demonstrated the trend.

The brightest students in science used to go into engineering and medicine. However, the brightest are no longer attracted to science and go into business. The next level of science students enter graduate school while the still less competent enter dentistry, physical therapy, and similar professions. Finally, those who cannot qualify for special training go into teaching. There are always exceptions and these are eagerly looked for by faculty but when a student arrives for counseling in science with a C average, he/she can be expected to be directed toward teaching.

This attitude is shameful in a time when teachers are in great demand. But it is largely the fault of the teachers themselves. Present data indicates 10 percent of teachers cannot add a column of numbers, 35 percent cannot convert metric system values into or from the English system, and 74 percent cannot calculate values in an algebraic equation. This lack of knowledge is reflected in half of all high school students who do not know the composition of a star and its relationship in composition to the earth, the moon, or a comet, 46 percent who are unaware heat is produced by combustion, and 88 percent who do not know the origin of plastics. And the situation will not improve shortly. Forty-four states report a shortage of science teachers primarily in mathematics, physics, and chemistry. In some states less than 50 percent of the teachers in those subjects were certified to teach in their assigned areas. Ways must be devised to encourage more students to go into the classroom and to provide cash incentives for teaching achievement. It has been suggested that more scientists or teachers serving on school boards would make an impression on the system.

Texas is a notable example of some states that are now testing teachers for competence in subject matter. The most recent tests found that more than 10 percent of teachers could not pass a simple test that almost 100 percent of students in the eighth grade in European or Japanese schools could pass with ease. The suggestions made by teachers' colleges will not help the situation. They propose that additional training to improve instruction consist of 6 hours in subject matter and 15 hours in educational methods. The reverse would be the best solution to produce educated teachers.

We need the brightest minds in the classroom. It is doubly unfortunate at the high school level that other considerations are placed above teaching, as we will discuss later. And in departments of education, emphasis is placed upon the training to be a teacher, not upon the subject to be taught.

The high school teacher should be well paid and relieved of the burden of administrative duties and after-hours trivia. We need a professional teaching system where the paperwork is delegated to assistants and the teacher is given time to learn about the modern trends in society and to advance in education. Of greater importance, he/she must understand science well enough to be able to impart the mystery and the methods of science to the beginning student. The situation might be eased by larger classes in high school rather than the conventional twenty-five students dictated by educational authorities. The Japanese turn out better trained students with fifty in each class. Furthermore, when the student reaches college he/she will be fortunate if first classes are not sized in the hundreds, especially in state schools. For these reasons alone, larger high school classes should not be a real disadvantage to the student who will go on to college, and this is the student to whom we should pay the most attention. As it is, the average high school graduate comes to college with a poor background. The high school today allows many electives, and the student can graduate without a base in science. Fortunately the present climate is now forcing high schools to adopt a more rigid curriculum and to bar students from extracurricular activities unless passing grades are maintained. Such improvement cannot be maintained unless we train the best minds to teach in secondary education as a profession. The foundations of a scientific career are launched in the classroom, and it is here we must make a start with competent teachers.

THE COLLEGE

The colleges are the backbone of a technical work force. They furnish the large part of all employees in white-collar industries and occupations and the graduate schools furnish a large portion of the scientists and technicians. It behooves the college-bound student to chose the best college.

Determining the ranking of various colleges and departments is not difficult. *U. S. News and World Report* publishes rankings of colleges and departments each year. The National Science Foundation and the National Research Council send questionnaires at regular intervals to the scientific community asking for a ranking of the departments in all sciences. This material is widely disseminated. The report shifts the order of colleges from time to time, but the ranks of the top ten or twenty departments do not change greatly. One hears disparaging remarks about the ranking system and why a particular department was not included on the list, but in general most educators would agree that the rankings are valid. It is perfectly true that an individual can go to a college not on the list and obtain promotion and pay and advancement in a chosen field, but it is much easier when one is able to say "I went to Harvard" as opposed to "I went to Southern Arkansas State Teachers College."

WHAT'S WRONG WITH EDUCATION

A.E. Fraley has written an interesting book entitled *Schooling and Innovation* dealing with attempts of the public schools to solve the problems of education of the young.[6] Unfortunately the book is largely an excuse of the school system with very little attempt to provide constructive criticism. Fraley points out, for example, that the schools are deficient in that they fail to teach the three Rs, they do not meet the needs of children and society, they do not provide equal opportunity, they do not teach democratic principles, and they do not create a better social order. In each case the blame is not placed on the schools but on the society in which we live. The point is not made that a good educational system beginning early enough might solve some of the problems. Fraley does point out that conflict between curricula as proposed by committees, school boards, and teachers are often at the root of the problem, and she implies time and money would solve most of the problems. Fraley confuses the issues as do most educa-tors. True, we should have a better society, and it must begin in the schools, but without a fundamental background in the three Rs, rhetoric about a better society must fall on deaf student ears. The book also points out the changes in the school systems from John Dewey, to the Gary plan, to the idea of a core curricu-lum, to the Ford Foundation attempts to remake school systems stressing the role of democracy, but failing to emphasize the need for a basic education. The modern educator insists on teaching by the concept method and is opposed to rote teaching, but the advocators fail to realize that no concept can be developed without some foundation of basic knowledge.

VALUE FOR MONEY

H. J. Aaron, the well-known economist and philosopher, has pointed out that money is not the major problem of the school system.[7] Real expenditure on schools has risen about 4 percent per year for twenty-five years and yet the quali-ty of education has decreased. During the same period of time student /teacher ra-tios decreased from twenty-five to one to eighteen to one, more than 50 percent of teachers obtained graduate degrees, and 50 percent had 15 years or more of teaching experience. Yet the SAT scores declined from 960 to about 905 during this period.

One of the problems Aaron pointed out is the bureaucracy. During the last twenty-five years, the nonteaching employees of school systems increased by 400 percent and are now more than 50 percent of the total employees.[8]

The distinguishing characteristics separating a good from a bad school sys-tem have not been determined. The major items appear to include academic pur-pose, educational leadership, and professionalism.

Bainbridge has examined the technology of training and education and makes several important points.[9] He says that there are three ways to train a worker: to develop skills which comprise manual dexterity and recognition of the task; to begin rule based training encouraging recognition of symbols, restricted action, and analysis; and finally, to develop knowledge based training creating an expert who can think for himself. The assembly line methods of American factories and schools teach only the first attributes. In another definition, the transition from novice worker to expert progresses along the same lines of skill, rules, and knowledge.

Such an analysis also redefines the training program. Training from the viewpoint of the company must involve three major attributes: acquisition of skills necessary for performance, optimization of system performance through education, and attitude alteration of the worker toward objectives of the com-pany. Failure of any one of the three can result in total failure. Again, the fail-ure of the automobile companies to enhance goal seeking by the workers, and with it attitude alteration, have created many of the problems.

The problem becomes more acute in a high tech system. Such a system creates greater demand for knowledge and less for skills. In such a system there is often no relationship between the processes the worker controls and the internal processes of the system. Consider the computer worker who does not understand the working of a mainframe computer.

In a technical position there is also no relationship between manual input and work output. Although accuracy of input is important, the internal manipulations are the determinants of output. At the same time, accuracy is important because the costs of a mistake may be very high in time and money. And finally, the worker often sees no results of the work—the time delay between input and output may be long. This creates a major demand for information flow in the system, so that workers are not isolated from the output and the system.

The average worker in technical systems may be required to know the machine, the data framework, the task required, and the interactions with other parts of the system in order to do a good job. The systems are rapidly changing, which in turn makes the knowledge-based system more complex. Process control, flexible production automation (FPA), and new control techniques demand a high skill level. The computer system invented in the United States and now being developed in Japan called "fuzzy logic" is a case in point.[10] In fuzzy logic systems, there are no black-and-white answers. Data input may be a series of variables changing with respect to each other. The computer checks all answers and predicts a probable result, but the operator must serve as interpreter.

Other systems analyze data and present information to the operator for decisions. HALO (Handling Alarms using Logic) takes information from 2,500 sensors in an alarm system, prioritizes the information and presents it a color code referring to degrees of urgency the operator must then understand.

The new systems also lead directly into training itself with interactive systems. These intelligent tutorial systems are capable of assessing a student's prior knowledge, problem learning area, ability, and preferences, and from these factors designing a learning program aimed at the specific needs of a company. Computer managed instruction (CMI), and PLATO, are examples of such systems. Obviously the design of such a system is a complex programming challenge. The program designers must be expert in the knowledge to be imparted, they must have information about the learner, they must be able to direct interactive processes as the learner interacts with the machine, and they must use natural language formatting so that learning a computer language does not interfere with the learning process.

MATHEMATICS—A DISMAL FAILURE

In any area of life, business, work in a fastfood restaurant, or as an engineer or scientist, mathematics is required. The ability to make change, to calculate percent, or to figure interest payments demands facility with numbers. Mathematics is useful on a personal basis, in the civics and political arena, as a professional requirement, for leisure and to develop cultural pursuits. It must be a part of every student's life. [10] Unfortunately, our students are not trained from grade school on to handle figures.

A recent report by the National Research Council, *Everybody Counts*, has highlighted the problems. [11] The council points out that the difficulty is not the lack of an innate mathematical ability in some students, but that students do not apply themselves, parents deprecate math as a subject, or teachers are incompetent. The report goes on to suggest that the situation can be turned for the better by a reasonable approach. However, the problems are compounded by a lack of knowledge about how to remedy the deficiency. All attempts by the educational community to date have been failures.

Further problems arise when the demographics are considered. At present, about 25 percent of whites and 50 percent of blacks fail to finish high school and therefore are deficient in math. [12] Yet the latter group with other minorities will comprise most of the additions to the work force by 1999. Only 15 percent will be white males. The demographics are also against the teacher. Statistics indicate that there will a massive shortage of mathematics teachers with no chance of remedy.

The way in which mathematics is taught is deplorable. It is important that elementary students gain a sense of numbers, but they are forced to learn arithmetic when calculators will replace most of the functions. Secondary schools should focus (as many now do) on the concepts of mathematics. Students should be taught the meaning of mathematics in everyday life rather than meaningless problems. A worker to be useful in society must know when to use mathematics and how to use it. This requires integration of knowledge rather than the step-by-step basic approach taught in many schools where minimal competency exams are used to test students. The methods of twenty-five years of curriculum development in mathematics have only taught us what not to do. We can end the discussion by summarizing the National Research Council's recommendations:

1. Develop a common core of math for all students.
2. Switch from teaching to learning.
3. Recognize the part that mathematics plays in society.
4. Develop a broad-based knowledge in students.
5. Develop use of computers and calculators.

An important point must be made here. Schools must learn to teach in a new way. Teaching *information,* the current method, is dated because the information changes on a day-to-day basis. On the other hand, teaching *knowledge,* how to apply information, has a lasting value.

We can turn our attention to other sciences as deplorable as mathematics. Students go through high school and much of college without a decent laboratory course in biology, physics, or mathematics. Teachers are scarce especially in physics, with chemistry trailing a close second. Biology teachers are in greater supply; but even here there will be a shortage within a few years. We lag behind other countries in the number of students who go to graduate school in the sciences. Our graduate schools in the hard sciences are filled with foreign students who are training at our expense. This may be a fine thing in a one-world society but at the moment it is reducing the United States to the status of a second rate power.

We can summarize the total effect by listing the findings of the Commission on Education published in *A Nation at Risk*:[12]

1. In nineteen academic tests in various fields the United States ranked no higher than third and in seven of the tests it ranked last in comparison with other countries.

2. There are 23 million functional illiterates in the country and 13 percent of all seventeen-year-olds are illiterate.

3. Standard achievement test scores are lower now than they were twenty six years ago.

4. SAT scores are dropping every year and have been for the past twenty years with only short periods of gain.

5. Maximum scores on the SAT have declined.

6. Among seventeen-year-olds 40 percent cannot draw inferences from data, yet this is critical to understanding quality control, production, and science.

7. Only 20 percent of high school students can write a coherent essay.

8. Only 30 percent can solve relatively simple math problems (see the discussion on math above).

9. In order to maintain standards colleges were forced to increase remedial classes 76 percent in five years.

10. The average student does less than one hour of homework each day.

11. The education system is concealing the true facts.

12. Average grades have been *rising* while average achievement is *falling*.

13. In thirteen states, a student can graduate with 50 percent elective courses.

14. Most developed countries require three times as much science for graduation as do American schools.

15. Education is further diluted by state laws requiring state-supported colleges to accept all high school graduates. This occurs in some 20 percent of all colleges.

EDUCATION—-AN EXAMPLE

The Boston Latin School is 350 years old. It was established in 1635 to provide for the education of future leaders of the country. Boston Latin School fulfilled the need and graduated such notables as Ralph Waldo Emerson, George Santayana, Theodore H. White, Leonard Bernstein, and John Adams. Admission was by examination and the curriculum was so tough that attrition averaged about 30 percent. But that may be changing. The NAACP has sued to have the school opened to all so it would become just another public high school in Boston. Nothing could be worse for education in the United States and nothing could more clearly demonstrate reverse discrimination. Boston Latin School for years has stood for quality education and has made the student toe the line or leave. To argue now that blacks have a right to attend the school without qualifications makes a farce of education in the United States at a time when all forces suggest more, not less education should be our goal.

Boston Latin School standards should reflect our own. We should be proud of a certain degree of elitism. No person and no nation can advance without it. Few would argue there would be little point in presenting a hack violinist on the same stage with Itzak Perlman, but these same persons would argue that a college or a high school should treat everyone in the same way. Elitism is as important in education as it is in arts or music where it has been accepted as a norm.

The elitist attitude is accepted in Japan and most countries of Europe where a series of tough examinations weed out the poorer student in grammar school and later in high school so that only those at the very highest levels of performance can expect to enter college. In stark contrast, our educational system has been geared to a least common denominator. We spend large sums of school funds on the "special" child and neglect the really special child, the gifted pupil. It has been said with some truth that the majority of all inventions and new ideas come from 5 percent of the population. It is these to whom we should pay attention. The Japanese and the European have long known this and the strict examination schedules they use from grade school to determine admission to college is an indication of their intentions.

Faith in common sense has been restored in part by the new "no pass —no play" rule in high schools in Texas and elsewhere. The aim of an educational system is to provide an education, not to create a championship football team. There should be no sympathy for the coaches who argue that a student will drop out of school unless he plays football and will thus get no education. He gets none anyway, and is expensive to the tax system. Elitism must extend to exclusion of sports if they interfere with education.

We must also have a high degree of prejudice against poor education. The reasons for poor education are due to two circumstance—one can be blamed on the pupils and one on the teachers. Let us reemphasize that the solution to these faults is not money. There is far too much money in the system for the amount of education we are receiving. The cost/benefit is dismal.

In the classroom today there is a mixture of races. The Asians dominate the class. The Semites, including the Jew, are second, the white races in general are third, and the blacks are fourth. The Asians are generally very good in mathematics and science and they have a great deal of family pressure to do well so their analytical skills bring them to the front. A low grade is a loss of face. The Boston Latin School confirms the observations. For many years there were no Asians in it. Within the last few years the school has become about 20 percent Asian and a large percent of them finish the curriculum. The blacks were admitted earlier, but there are still only 10 percent blacks and 80 percent drop out before graduation. This is not the fault of the whites, the Asians, or the Latin Americans. It is the fault of the blacks. There is no discrimination in these statements, although the black races will inevitably take that position. There is no question but that everyone should have the same opportunity, but beyond the point, everyone should make it on his own. In fact, one may notice in some locations that prejudice against Asians is now beginning to approach that which blacks suffered in the 1930s, yet they are still moving upward.

We hasten to accuse other races. The white majority has a lack of educational drive. In the earlier decades of this century, until the student revolution of the 1960s, students were largely white, well dressed, polite, and industrious. The 1960s produced students who were bearded, unkempt, and more interested in political activity than study, and the quality of education decreased markedly. The situation is slowly turning around but few white students now have the motivation and family drive found among Asians. In fact we have had complaints from whites as well as blacks about the Asians dominating the classes. Both the whites and blacks should get the same answer, "You have the same instructor, book, and time. Compete."

The population as a whole is demanding a social balance in schools, overeducation of the lower levels of intelligence and maintenance of some educational institutions whose standards are far below those of other schools. We must demand a benefit in good education in return for the cost paid by industry for poor education, and by everyone else in the form of taxes.

By the same token, we should object to bilingual education. In a large city school we have some forty languages spoken and there are many more Asian languages than Spanish. Industry where everyone must understand and respond to the same ideas and concepts cannot afford a multilanguage system. The money for education can be more wisely spent on better teachers and better schools. It could be pointed out that recent winners of the National Spelling Bee have been Asians with three years or so of residency in the United States who were not in a bilingual program. The major objection is that English is not well taught as a first language yet we strain to teach it as a second language in our schools. Arriving college students of all races graduate from our high schools unable to write a correct sentence, unable to spell, and unable to express themselves adequately. Nothing is more frustrating than to talk to a modern student whose every other word is "Yuh know. Yuh know." Most colleges are now giving exit examinations to all students to be sure they can read and write English before graduating from college, a direct comment on our educational system.

Even a cursory reading of this chapter should convince us we must make major changes in the educational system, and we must begin at once. The book, *A Nation at Risk,* a report on the state of the nation's schools issued several years ago, has understated the case—we are now more at risk. Those states that have made an attempt to reverse the situation have found that money alone will not solve the problem; there needs to be a completely new approach to the aims of education at all levels. When M.H. McCormack wrote the book, *What They Don't Teach You at Harvard Business School* he pointed out the problems in business education where the student is not trained for the real business world. They are no different from problems in other forms of education.[12]

SCHOOLS AND PRIORITIES

Despite the overall shortage of scientists, the demand for the scientists varies from year to year. At the time of this writing there is considerable demand for engineers and geologists but almost none for biologists. There is certainly very little demand for the biologist who is not trained in a specific technique.

However, the changing oil market is now affecting the employment of geologists, who may soon be in increasing demand. The engineers have always had a reasonable level of employment, but demand for specific types of engineers has varied from year to year. At the moment there is demand for electronics trainees but not as much demand for mechanical engineers except for those working in control processes. Computer scientists are still in demand, but interest seems to be decreasing somewhat.

The increasing impact of the oil industry on the energy picture is increasing the demand for chemical engineers. Biologists have been in very great oversupply for some years, but the new biotechnology development in genetic engineering may well arouse more interest in some specific areas of engineering and biology. The next decade may see an entirely different mix and only a good general education in science can prepare anyone for the work needs of the future.

The one relatively stable profession is medicine. Over the years most physicians have managed to maintain a practice and to make a good income but even here the trend of the times indicates more stringency as control on the cost of health care increases. The payment of health care costs by industry may be affected by these trends.

Nevertheless, the overall trend is clear. Each science increases in complexity on an exponential curve and the time required for the individual to obtain information and put it to practical use also increases. The pace of science in general is accelerating all the time, and the time between discovery and application is shortening each decade as communication becomes freer and the crossbreeding between sciences increases. Education must keep pace.

As an example, a biologist is not much of a scientist unless he/she is also acquainted in a more than trivial fashion with mathematics, physics, and chemistry. As a result, demand for workers with bachelor's degrees decreases and for those with an advanced degree increases. A student in an area such as medical technology or biology will usually be able to obtain a position, but will never head the organization. Nowadays such positions are always held by someone with an advanced degree. Therefore, it behooves the young man or woman entering college to consider carefully the choices in a career in science.

One major event taking place may well affect the extent of on-the-job training provided by employers. The trend in most universities is to eliminate the laboratories in the hard sciences. Hands-on experience is the only way to develop innovation as the student sees the actual object under study and the way it works. The pressure of interest groups against the use of live animals, the high costs of laboratory instruction, and the resistance of the professors to the time required have effectively eliminated the laboratory in many universities, especially in the freshman and sophomore courses.

The restriction in laboratory study reached a high point in engineering schools a few years ago when many schools switched to engineering science and dropped laboratories in circuit design, power plants, and similar applied topics. Complaints from industry that students were knowledgeable in theory but were unable to do anything has partially reversed the trend. We may yet see the same reversal in other sciences that are neglecting laboratories.

The situation is particularly acute in medicine, where many of the classical laboratories using human or animal experimentation have been dropped in favor of computer-assisted learning modules. If the laboratories are also dropped in high school and college, where will the knowledge be obtained? We must educate the general public about the values of a scientific education apart from the fads of nonscientists.

MEDICAL EDUCATION IN THE UNITED STATES

As we have remarked, provision of health care for employees is a major cost factor in any industry both for the industry and the employee. One of the reasons for high health costs is the way physicians are educated. The United States may have the best medical care in the world; it certainly has the costliest. The cost of medical care continues to rise at more than twice the annual rise in the cost of living. The reason is very simple. The medical school faculty trains students in their own image with the latest and most expensive techniques. In addition the physician is respected in our society, and this encourages specialization thus adding to medical costs.[13]

Medical schools have paid little attention to the needs of a changing population. For example, reliable estimates are that 50 percent of all hospital beds will be occupied by geriatric patients within a few years, but the medical schools provide almost no training in geriatrics.

The medical student is trained in hospital practice and in its effective use, yet 85 percent or more of practice will be outside the hospital and the diseases treated will be totally different. The geriatric patient, increasing rapidly in numbers and need for medical care, also has a totally different spectrum of disease. The physician leaves the hospital trained in some specialty, and this specialty bears no relation to need. The estimated needs in the population are for about seven internists or general practitioners to each surgeon, but the actual numbers are closer to two to one, suggesting a vast oversupply of surgeons with resulting higher prices, occupation of operating rooms and hospitals, and unnecessary surgery.

The training of the young physician is an expensive process. The average medical school has expenses ranging upward of $100,000 per year for each student. A large part of this cost, borne by the taxpayer, is wasteful expenditure of funds. The faculty-student ratio in most medical schools is almost one to one while in most universities the ratio may be as large as twenty to one and the average student costs about $3,000 per year. The faculty has expensive labs, equipment, and facilities, teaches a few hours a year, and usually has little or no training in how to teach.

The medical student is encouraged to specialize even though the real demand at present is for the general practitioner. Some 85 percent of medical students choose a specialty and about 30 percent chose surgery in spite of the oversupply. The medical schools do little to limit the choices, although alternatives are available.

Medical students are trained in the medical school to use technology, usually to excess. Surgeons perform about 150,000 cardiac bypass operations per year although evidence suggests many patients could be treated with drugs alone. Some three times as many caesarean sections are performed in the United States as are performed in other countries with the same infant mortality rate. In fact, studies in Sweden suggest that infants do better with natural delivery. Much of the excess surgery is due to the oversupply of surgeons.

Because physicians are so taught in the medical school, the overuse of drugs for treatment is a chronic condition of our medical system. And again, the need for drugs and the type of drugs in the geriatric patient is vastly different from that of the general population, but this is not stressed in medical schools.

We now have a medical bill of about $2,200 per year for every man, woman, and child in the country and much of the cost is due to the way medical students are trained. We could generalize about the problems of medical education now costing the taxpayer billions of dollars each year:

1. Objectives of the medical school should be stated precisely and concisely. The kind of physicians to be produced and how they will be

trained should be specified.

2. The curriculum should reflect the needs of the patient now and for the immediate future.

3. Specialty training should be subordinate to general practice.

4. Students should be taught economics, psychology, and social sciences as a part of medical training.

Such a revision of the curriculum would produce a physician at a cheaper cost, more oriented toward the patient, and trained in the medicine of the future.

Education is the backbone of our society. It produces an educated electorate, a competent work force, and innovations to develop the future. Without it we are a third-rate nation. With it we can again compete for first class. Time is running out. A whole generation of educationless students has been created, and another generation is beginning. If we do not act now to upgrade teachers, curriculum, and schools it will soon be too late to save still another cohort of students.

A CRITICAL SUMMARY

We have stressed science education as a major problem. The problem exists in all forms of education. The state of Texas has recently tried to alleviate the situation by requiring that all seniors in high school or entering college freshmen take the Texas Academic Skills Program (TASP) exam testing reading, writing, and mathematics ability on a very low level. Furthermore, the law requires the colleges to provide remedial education for all who fall below the minimum. This highly mistaken idea should be properly buried. Colleges can not properly train the future generations of scientists and mathematicians we desperately need and at the same time provide remedial education for a group of illiterates. This is properly the job of elementary and high schools and their school boards. Their feet should be held to the fire until a better education is provided the youngsters. The desperate problem is highlighted by the present estimate of the state of Texas that up to 90 percent of blacks and 50 percent of whites will fail the exam and require the remedial courses. We cannot produce a work force that can compete in the world markets without a complete turn-around of the educational system.

It is imperative that industry demand standards of the school system to produce a quality workman. Pressure can be applied through the force of taxation. Industry as a whole pays a large portion of all taxes and thus should have a say. Industry can help in other ways. Experts in various fields can be loaned to the school system, magnet schools can be encouraged in areas of interest to business, funds can be provided to develop new curricula, and books and instruments can be donated to laboratories. For example, organization of consortia for development of educational ideas between academia and industry could be encouraged.

Consortia can be set up between schools and industry to set standards and motivate students. Industrial executives can make a commitment to education by running for election to school boards to have a direct influence on the trends of education. Business must be committed to higher standards in education. While it is true that industry can and does provide education for workers after they are employed, this is an expensive and time-consuming process to make up for the deficiencies that could have been avoided by proper instruction at the high school level.

REFERENCES

1.   National Geographic Society, *Knowledge of Geography* (preprint). Washington, D.C.: National Geographic Society Press, 1989.
2.   D. M. Topolnicki, "Your Stake in Local Schools," *Money* 19 (5):84 (May 1990).
3.   M. N. Baily, "Productivity in a Changing World," *Brookings Institution* 16:1 (1981).
4.   J. D. Lewis, "Technology, Enterprise, and American Economic Growth," *Science* 215:1204 (1982).
5.   L. L. Lederman, "Science and Technology Policies and Priorities," *Science* 237:1125 (1987).
6.   A. E. Fraley, *Schooling and Innovation.* New York: Tyler Gibson, 1981.
7.   H. J. Aaron, ed., *Setting National Priorities.* Washington, D.C.: Brookings Institution, 1990.
8.   J. E. Chubb and T. M. Moe, *Politics, Markets, and America's Schools.* Washington, D.C.: Brookings Institution, 1990.
9.   L. Bainbridge and S. A. R. Quintanilla, eds., *Developing Skills with Information Technology.* New York: John Wiley and Sons, 1989.
10.   K. Self, "Designing with Fuzzy Logic," *IEEE Spectrum* 27 (11):42 (November 1990).
11.   National Research Council, *Everybody Counts.* Washington, D.C.: National Academy Press, 1989.
12.   M. H. McCormack, *What They Don't Teach You at Harvard Busiess School.* New York: Bantam Books, 1984.
13.   J. H. U. Brown, "Medical Schools in Crisis," *Evaluation and the Health Professions* 11:147 (1988).

7
Excellence in the Workplace

A major change is occurring in the way the personnel of an organization are treated by the management and the way they respond. There is little need to rehash the quality circle theory and other methods originated by Americans and developed by the Japanese but other trends must be addressed. Brophy and Walsh found some 25 million workers are now part-time.[1] Where an organization once filled positions with full-time workers the trend is now to part-time work.[2] And this can be both an advantage and a disadvantage to the employer.

But other problems are arising in the workplace. In recent years factories have found that maintenance of the inventory in a "just-in-time" mode, where delivery to the production floor is made as the material is needed, is cheaper and faster than maintaining a large inventory all the time. This could reduce the need for stockroom employees, and CEOs are beginning to find that the same idea may be applied to the other workers. Computer operators, stenographers, and others may be hired as needed from firms specializing in supplying office workers. It has been estimated that one of four employees is a "just-in-time" worker. Some estimates suggest the number of such workers will grow by 80 percent in the next ten years, meaning about one of every two or three employees would be temporary. The major disadvantage is that the worker cannot be trained to standards of quality production on a temporary basis or cannot be educated to the needs of the industry because there is no incentive to learn the business. The employer hires skills of typing or filing or computer input without regard to future needs or aims of the company.

There is a major advantage to the industry in using part-time workers. There is no requirement for raises or for benefits or pensions, and there is no union problem. Overhead is reduced. No recruiting is necessary, and with many firms now specializing in the provision of part-time employees there is no hiring.

The employees are furnished as needed under contract. The disadvantage lies in the old argument about company loyalty and development of specializations. However, few modern companies inspire great company loyalty (how can they when CEOs move every three years?), and the temporary jobs are clerical, steno-graphic, and routine maintenance requiring no specialization.

This new approach naturally generates disquiet among employees. Surveys of employer and employee attitudes illustrate the point very well.[3] They point out the Fortune 500 companies have less employee satisfaction and less innova-tion than smaller companies. The larger companies have a greater hierarchy gap—the difference between the lowest salaries and the highest is very great and this creates dissatisfaction among the lower workers. Few workers believe the company shares success with workers, that the company listens to the workers, or that their jobs are rewarded. This study suggests that the only way to elimi-nate the problem is to share aims and goals of the company with the employee, share information, and share success. But this requires a reeducation of the work force and the CEO. The Japanese learned long ago that the worker and the indus-try must be closely related to common goals and the future. The American CEO assumes that the goals of workers are his goals, but this is not usually the case unless the worker has become a part of the company decisions and plans. Hartman and Pearlstein point out a senior executive in a Fortune 500 company who stated, "I'm alone at the top and I deserve the rewards."[3] He failed to under-stand that without employees dedicated to quality and the company goals, there would be no success from which to gain rewards.

The Bureau of Labor Statistics suggests that although the extent of unem-ployment is still about 6 percent there is every indication that this is a false number. The rate is high because of unemployment among teenagers, unskilled, and unemployable workers while it is low (5 percent) among the real workers and as low as 2.5 percent among managers, again demonstrating the education factor. A slowly growing population together with the ever-aging trained work force will drive the demand for workers to new levels.

At the same time that the skills required of the work force are increasing, the educational level of the worker may actually be decreasing. Each year 500,000 students drop out of school, and 70,000 of those who graduate may not be able to read their diplomas. Skill levels are falling, and most companies are forced to adopt new training and educational programs in order to produce barely useful employees. And in a technological age where there is a computer on al-most every desk top and machines are computer-controlled in the workplace, the problem is compounded. The situation is acute. Chemical Bank has reported that previously 75 percent of job applicants taking a simple test in mathematics and English were able to pass the exam, but the scores are now so low that the pass rate is down to 55 percent. It has been estimated that 22 percent of current jobs require a college education, but some 30 percent will require such training in the future while the need for high school graduates will actually drop. As we report-ed in the last chapter, if we do not properly train high school students, they are unlikely to go on to college or to succeed once they arrive. By the

1990s we will have a deficit of workers because the age of the baby boom has passed. Unfortunately the signs are those of workers who will demand higher wages because of scarcity, but will not be trained to hold any meaningful positions in an age of technology. Something must be done at once.[4],[5]

It has been estimated that a part of the decline in productivity is due to younger workers without basic language and math skills. At a time when higher levels of training are needed in the workplace a large portion of all engineering students are foreigners on temporary student visas (Fig. 7-1).

The bright, mathematically minded students are going into business rather than engineering. And their training may be wasted. We have many more managers in business than we need. Our need now and for the foreseeable future is for workers on the floor, engineers, technicians, and skilled workers of many kinds. Many prospective employees with a college education have none of the skills needed in the workplace. College training in the arts or in general topics provides no background for a technical business. The number of individuals graduating with a degree in science is small and shows no sign of increasing.

As a result companies are turning to the older employee to remain on the job, trying to retain trained women by providing job benefits such as child care, and adopting other measures to retain a trained work force. Such problems usually result in one answer—raise salaries to attract the lower-level worker. But as salaries increase, and profits decrease, companies are resorting to part time employees, as mentioned above, to reduce costs. This also affects the stability of the work force.

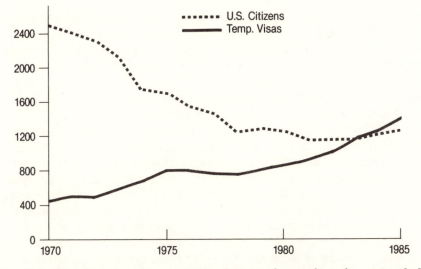

Fig. 7-1. The increase in graduate degrees in engineering awarded to foreign temporary visa holders as compared to U.S. citizens [*Technological Dimensions of International Competitiveness.* Washington, D.C.: National Academy Press, 1988.]

These discussions suggest that the organization must begin to look to the long-term future rather than short-term profits if it is to succeed in an atmosphere where job seekers are scarce and ill-trained. Output may depend upon ability to recruit a new breed of worker who is trained in some technical field. It may be necessary to develop programs to train workers, keep them happy and retain them in the company for longer periods.

Keeping workers happy takes more than salary and vacations. The use of computers permits close surveillance of the worker, keeps a constant tab on his activities, and creates an attitude of "Big Brother is watching you" resented by many workers.[6] Further specialization of jobs with the tighter control it brings also brings about boredom. The CEO must develop a new attitude toward office management.

It must be remembered that resentment at the bottom of the employment scale is a characteristic of all large companies. However, incentive pay, promotion, and recognition can erase some of the prejudice. The resentment is particularly severe in the health care industry where the lower-level worker is poor in comparison to the relatively wealthy physician with whom he/she may work closely. It is almost as bad in education where superintendents make high salaries while the teachers are paid a bare living wage. Again education may turn the direction to a more favorable outcome. The schools in Chicago have adopted a plan where the teachers, parents, and other concerned parties will have an input into selection of boards, teachers, curriculum, and other matters. This will require intensive education of the entire system to allow reasonable choices to be made.

Two other major personnel problems face the CEO. The best estimates today are that about 10 percent of workers are employed in checking, quality control, and inspection, an employment of about 600,000 workers. The trend is toward the robot that can perform control procedures accurately and rapidly. Some estimates are that more than one-half of all inspectors will be replaced by robots, a loss of 300,000 jobs. The CEO is faced with wholesale firing, retraining of employees, or steps to appease the work force.[5] Improvement in quality may also result in a decrease in the number of inspectors. The Japanese have partly resolved the question of quality by placing it in the hands of the individual so that fewer inspectors are needed. In Germany, the cost of an item includes close quality control but as a result little repair is needed after the product reaches the sales floor or the customer, and continued inspection at all levels of manufacture can be discontinued. But again this requires education of the worker to identify standards and to make the necessary adjustments to keep standards high.

In a second area, industry is faced with the problem of general education. Some large companies spend as much as $100 million per year educating workers to do simple tasks in mathematics, to use computers and to understand simple organization of materials.[1] The problem is likely to grow worse rather than better. The modern machine, the use of computers in the office, and the development of more sophisticated methods of accounting demand a worker who has skills in mathematics, English, and analysis of complex problems.

The United States is training fewer of these individuals each year. We are no longer able to compete with the Japanese, the English, and the Germans or with other countries in providing a work force that is highly skilled and can be further trained to perform complex operations. The SAT scores in our high schools are not rising. Asians, who are a small minority of the population, excel in the college classrooms. The majority of graduate students in engineering and science are foreign. We must do something at once.

As a further incentive, American business is sending most of the piece work, simple tasks, and routine line operations abroad where labor is cheap and repetition is accepted. Consequently, the jobs left at home become more and more sophisticated and workers must be better trained to perform them. Many companies have started schools to educate workers in the basics and many industries send engineers and other critical personnel to graduate school at company expense in return for a period of employment. The executive must enter into the politics and control of education if he/she is to have a work force in the future.

As the blue-collar worker shrinks in number, service industries grow rapidly. It is estimated that 70 percent of all workers are now in some form of service (Fig. 7-2).[4]

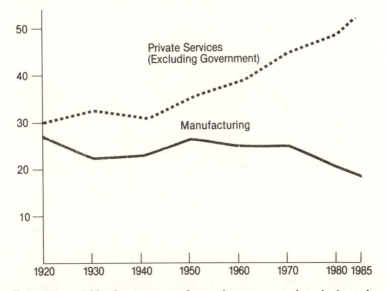

Fig. 7-2. The shift from manufacturing to service industries (National Academy of Engineering, *Technological Dimensions of International Competitiveness* Washington, D.C.: National Academy of Science Press, 1988)

The distressing fact is that 80 percent of all hirings in 1987 were in service industries, and manufacturing actually lost workers. As we have remarked earlier, services contribute almost nothing to the GNP and nothing to producing goods that can be exported.

In fact it has been estimated that switching a worker from manufacturing to service reduces his contribution to the GNP by 40 percent. Services usually require a greater number of managers per worker. This also tends to decrease the productivity of the system. On the other hand, most service industries require less skilled workers and less training in order to obtain a satisfactory performance. In an era of poor education, such companies may be better off.

The service industries may be harming the total economy in several ways. One of the services is the provision of legal advice. Legal service is a zero sum game absorbing countless hours with no results. When a company loses a suit, it must pay without any compensation through new output. That we are a litigious society is beyond question, but it should be a matter of shame rather than pride.

Most other countries appear to maintain society with much less legal input. Legal action decreases total output of the company and the GNP. Here education may be a disadvantage to society. Law schools are overproducing lawyers much as the business schools are overproducing MBAs, and neither contributes to the GNP.

Medical care also suffers from the same problems of increasing service without a compensatory return on investment. The cost of the same medical care increases at a rate greater than the cost of living because of overtraining and specialization of medical personnel.

Changes are coming. Employers are switching to pay for knowledge rather than by the job or longevity and other nontraditional payment schemes are beginning to develop.[7] But Sanoff claims that machines intimidate the present ill-trained workers and causes them to feel that they are responding to the machine, not to the real world. The solution, Sanoff feels, is for everyone to become some kind of manager, albeit in a minor role.[8] Sanoff is wrong on one score. To date, the machine has not reduced the work force.[9] The vast amounts of data produced by the machine on a daily or weekly basis, when it was previously available only monthly or quarterly, has increased the need for clerical personnel. Between 1977 and 1982, real production rose 8 percent, while clerical employment rose 15 percent and white-collar employment rose 18 percent. Banks, the most completely automated of all industries, increased employment 21 percent from 1977 to 1982, while productivity fell 2 percent (Fig.7-3).

As a corollary, the demand for accountants is rising steadily despite automation of most accounting procedures. Other hidden drags on the economy are reducing productivity. Almost one million persons are employed as security forces. This contributes nothing to the GNP. Of course, such a force requires little or no education and little training.

More and more executives are producing less and less work. In an earlier illustration, it was pointed out that when an automobile company reduced executive staff by 20 percent, production increased by 30 percent. Firms are turning to

machines to replace workers and this may be all to the good if it is done carefully. But the replacement of cheap workers by expensive machines may not be a
good trade. The Japanese have found that the worker and the machine are inseparable. In fact they have said, "Our machines do not break down," an indication
of the close tie between man and machine and an indication of the training required for the worker to maintain the machine at all times, not just when it
needs repairs.

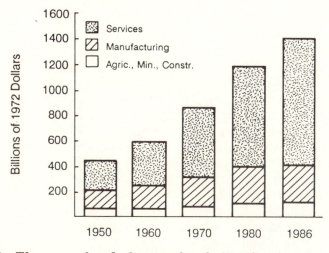

Fig. 7-3. The growth of the service industries in real dollars
(Taken from Guile and Quinn, *Managing Innovation*.Washington, D.C.:National
Academy Press, 1988.)

Still another problem looms on the horizon. The labor force is not only uneducated, but in 1980 we were seeing the result of the baby boom that follows
all wars with a correspondingly large entry into the work force of approximately
25 million workers between the ages of sixteen and twenty four.[10] By 1995 it
is estimated that only 21 million potential employees will be available in the
same time period.

When this is compared to the estimated 120 million jobs in the economy,
the shortfall is obvious. Furthermore, the job market will shift to different skill
demands. Computer operators, medical assistance personnel, and systems analyst
positions will all grow more rapidly than other sections of the economy, and
these demand special training. The other growth areas are in low-paying jobs
such as retail sales, drivers, and clerks.[7]

The United States as a whole will soon suffer from major employment dis-
ruptions. At the moment the population of California is 42 percent Hispanic,
black, or Asian and the ratio is certain to increase. The rural population is rapidly becoming a minority group as well. The group as a whole (some Asians excluded) have a high dropout rate in school, and can take only low-paying un-

skilled jobs. This can only decrease the GNP as this large force demands places in the work force.

Moreover, the problem cannot be solved easily because it is an international one. The present projections indicate that the European Economic Community will decrease in population from 330 million to about 310 million in the next forty years with a resultant decrease in its labor force. One of the highest producing countries in Europe, Germany, will see a decrease in population from 61 million to 45 million with no chance of providing the work force to maintain output. The end result is that the only supply of labor will be from the Southern Hemisphere and the LDCs. Some estimates are 950 of every 1,000 employables will be from the LDCs within the next forty years. And this group is largely uneducated, untrained, and represents a serious loss of productivity.

At one time we could rely on importation of skilled workers from central Europe, but the only reliable supply is now Mexico, South America, and Africa, creating problems of training and maintenance. Furthermore, the demographics of the situation may create strains in international and national relations. As the population of the more developed countries ages, there will be a different mix of requirements. Foodstuffs, entertainment, kinds of automobiles, alternate transportation, cosmetics, building standards, and clothing requirements will all change, and business must change with them. The day of appealing to the eighteen-year-old and the Yuppie is past or soon will be. In fact, commercial television is beginning to reflect the change by appealing to older persons with new programs and new advertisements. An unfortunate consequence may be a conflict between the unskilled younger workers and the older population. Younger workers with lower wage scales because of lack of training resent the older better educated workers and will attempt to replace them by sheer weight of numbers. [10]

Industry is susceptible to the replacement of the higher-paid older workers with less well-paid younger workers who can be trained do the same job. But as the number of elderly increases, it may become feasible to retrain them in other positions so that they may continue to contribute to the work force beyond the normal retirement age. The wise manager must look to the future in terms of type of employee, and how that employee will be found and trained. The costs will undoubtedly increase as the demand for workers increases and supply decreases. These problems are complicated by the fact that most employers do not understand their workers and therefore are unable to motivate them properly in order to obtain more productivity. [11] The answer may lie in the shift of kind of employees and the jobs they do. Extension of the lifetime working period may become essential. This will require motivation and training of individuals who now retire at the earliest possible age to avoid the drudgery of present jobs. The elderly worker may have to be trained to work on labor-saving devices or to work at home to minimize effort. Women may become a more integral part of the work force.

Such an approach will require restructuring benefit packages. We are now creating child care centers for working women. A recent demand is the creation of care centers for the elderly. IBM, AT&T, and others have already begun to enter the field. Such service will increase the costs of health care to the employer. Chrysler now pays about $550 per year for health care of its employees, and Rashi Fein has suggested that a system of adequate health care, borne in part by industry, would cost about $1,560 per employee. This would add about eighty cents per hour to the cost of wages, and in the lower paid industries (fast foods) this is an unacceptable increase in costs especially when added to the suggested increase in the minimum wage scales. Nevertheless, pressures for greater benefits are already being felt.[7]

Surveys of employers suggest that they may have the wrong priorities for the future.[11] Some 57 percent consider finances to be the most critical area, 40 percent consider personnel to be critical, and some 23 percent consider planning to be important. Almost none mentioned long-range planning, technology, or new techniques as the critical areas to increase competitiveness. The attitude continued to be expressed in answers to other questions. Employers considered management of information to be the most critical part of their jobs with personnel in second place.

Yet the managers are not as a whole trained to manage information, to use computers, or to use technology to the greatest benefit. We need to train a new generation of managers with different priorities.

It does not require clarification to place academia, health care systems, or the government in the picture presented above. The situation is particularly desperate in health care where the dichotomy between classes of workers is obvious. The professionals form one class distinct from the workers on one hand and the administrators on the other. The middle class in the health care system, the nurses, are considered to be professional by the nurses themselves and somewhat less so by the physician. And new classes of well-trained technicians working on complex instruments such as scanning devices, heart lung apparatus, and other highly technical patient support systems are rapidly developing and demanding privileges as professionals. The schism has led to a rapid withdrawal of nurses with the resulting shortage decreasing the level of care provided. The nurses want to assume more responsibility for the patient, which the physician is reluctant to relinquish in a time of decreasing patient loads and therefore decreasing incomes. The professional medical personnel generally refuse to take on-demand positions even though good scheduling and careful queuing theory could markedly improve health care costs.

The teacher is in a similar position. The teacher in Asia and Europe is accorded great respect and standing in the community even though salaries may not be high. In the United States the status is much lower. Part of the difficulty may be the fault of the teacher. Teachers poorly trained in subject matter cannot win the respect of pupils or families. Although salaries have been increasing, they are still low in proportion to the demands and the levels of education required. This again may be reflected in the opinion of teachers in general in the community. In addition, present-day teachers are not computer literate on the whole, but students who are turned out from training institutions must be able to operate relatively sophisticated machines. While the cash registers in fastfood stores are really computers, they are designed as "idiot boxes," but this cannot be counted on to continue into the future. The staff and the administration of the school systems must be prepared to develop new approaches to education as is happening to a small extent in the magnet schools specializing in training for particular occupations.

In addition, education management is not all that it could be. Superintendents in schools are trained in education in schools of education; their business experience and their academic experience may be woefully lacking. Administrators in hospitals are usually trained in business schools, and may not fully understand the health care system and how it works.

THE WORKER AND THE MILITARY

A major crisis of labor is arising. As the cold war winds down and military requirements lessen, a crisis of employment will develop. Hundreds of thousands of workers have spent a career working in military establishments on highly specific projects that will not translate well into a civilian economy. The airframe manufacturers, now facing a decrease in orders, are already laying off thousands of workers, and as the need for tanks, guns, and other armaments decreases, additional thousands will lose their jobs. They have skills that are highly developed but are almost useless.[13]

Some 30 percent of engineers and scientists in the country are employed by the military and many will be unable to find jobs. The military has expended $3 trillion in the last ten to fifteen years, and the decrease in national product occasioned by a decrease in military spending may well trigger a major recession.

H.R.101, recently passed by Congress has attempted to start identifying civilian products that can be produced in military establishments, identifying personnel who can be transferred to civilian occupations, and attempting to stave off the impact of military cutbacks. The impact is unknown.

Proposals have been made to use the defense employees who are trained in heavy industry to rebuild the infrastructure of the country; and this may be one solution if funds can be found. However, it is unlikely that defense employees can receive the high salaries they were paid on a cost plus basis by defense contractors.

The problem is not simple. Zraket states that of the $40 billion in military R and D only $0.9 billion is in basic research and $2.4 billion in exploratory development.[13] The rest of the R and D budget is used for test and evaluation of military equipment. Such skills may be of little value in the future. Ling, a well-known innovator, has suggested that the transferability of technology from government laboratories to industry is low, and we are supporting R and D that does not contribute to the national economy. He suggests closer cooperation between government R and D and the private, nonmilitary sectors of the economy.[12] Such an approach might help the transition.

THE MANAGER AS PERSONNEL

One area in which we have been negligent is training the manager. A graduate from the average business school is considered to be a manager by definition, but the background to manage a technical operation, as most industry is rapidly becoming, is totally lacking. In addition, the manager must learn to manage power and to use it properly, another attribute that the educational system does not provide.

Hiring a senior manager is part of the personnel problem of every organization, and the correct choice may make the difference between a productive and a nonproductive company. Every company would like a sure-fire test to identify correctly the person most likely to succeed as a manager. Great effort has been exercised to develop tests aimed at such identifications. Most have not been very successful.

Management textbooks outline the most desirable characteristics of managers. All are very similar. They are usually grouped into categories needing no explanation: physical characteristics, background, intelligence, personality, drive, and social responsibility.

Ghiselli has researched the problem extensively.[14] His findings are similar to the list above. He found these characteristics have not been uniformly successful in predicting leadership ability, and as a result many investigators have turned to the measurement of behavior rather than the attempt at identification and measurement of these listed characteristics. No scale has been devised to estimate accurately the value of background or the degree of social responsibility of a prospective manager.

Behavior has been evaluated on a variety of scales, but in general all measurement suffers from a lack of quantification. The managerial grid of Blake and Mouton was the standard method a few years ago.[15] This method assumed all managers could be ranked on a space grid ranging from an extremely person-oriented individual on one corner to an extremely task-oriented person on the other with various degrees of mixture in between. The difficulty is that successful managers have been found in all squares of the grid. The obvious best choice is a person who has the optimum regard for both the task and the people.

Difficulties in assessing leadership on such a scale have resulted in many variations on the theme. Proposals have been made to evaluate leadership on the basis of the situation the leader faces.[16] Some tests have attempted to rank situations facing the manager and determine the correct response to each in terms of the appropriate kind of leadership. The factors involved are grouped into leadership, subordinate relations, structure of tasks by the executive, and power of the leader. On the basis of these interactions, it has been decided that most leadership be grouped into permissive or directive attitudes. Such an approach leads to two possible solutions to any situation: the leader must change behavior to fit the situation, or the leader must change the situation to fit his concepts. However, none of the methods has been successful in predicting performance of managers to date. And no educational system has been developed to train managers in each category.

Recently a new method of classification has been advanced. This merely represents another in a long line of evaluation schemes and there is no indication that it will be any more successful than the others. This method, the Myer-Briggs Type Indicator (MBTI), asks about one hundred questions of the test taker and ranks the answers into sensing or intuitive personality types. It then breaks these down into sixteen patterns of behavior.[17] There is little need to recount all sixteen personality types here but a few examples will suffice:

1. An **ISTJ** (**I**ntroverted, **S**ensing, **T**hinking, **J**udging) type is the typical financial executive or accountant.

2. An **ENTP**(**E**xtroverted, **I**ntuitive, **T**hinking, **P**erceiving) type is interested in innovation and hates routine. They are entrepreneurs, not corporate executives.

3. An **INTJ** (**I**ntroverted, **I**ntuitive, **T**hinking, **J**udging) type makes an ideal CEO.

4. An **ESTJ** (**E**xtroverted, **S**ensing, **T**hinking, **J**udging) type is the general manager type.

It is apparent that the sales manager can be separated from a shop manager, who in turn can be differentiated from the planner and the scientist if such descriptions are valid. But again there is no attempt to determine whether the manager can manage technology and innovation.

Building teams with groups who understand the characteristics of other members of the group as defined by these personality types has been reputed to be highly successful. However, some managers consider the scheme to be like a religious revival that will disappear like the other evaluation fads.

Kanter interviewed several hundred CEOs about the characteristics they looked for in hiring or promoting an associate.[18] She found that overwhelmingly, the CEO hired staff members on the basis of personal chemistry between the associate and himself. She could find no evidence that any measure of competence was used in the assessment. This may be an indictment of the American system, especially since most other industrial countries appear either to train their executives for the job, or to look for professional competence in their background. Prospective Japanese managers spend years in the plants, learning the business, so professional competence is assured. American CEOs, in contrast, are often chosen from financial or management ranks without experience in the products of the company or its operations. In our time of conglomerates, the diversity of products in a single company or organization contributes to the lack of knowledge about the aims of the company and its long-term goals.

For these reasons, it is much more important that the American executive learn to understand foreign counterparts than to understand contemporaries at home. While American business culture is fairly homogeneous, the variety among foreign companies is enormous. As a single cultural example, and others could be chosen among Europeans, Indians, and so on, the Japanese have a totally different approach.

1. The Japanese deal in ambiguity while the United States attempts to pin down all of the details of an operation.

2. The Japanese tend to use language that is vague and general as opposed to the precise definitions Americans require.

3. Communication is direct between Americans but very indirect and often confusing with the Japanese.

4. Integrity in the American industry is precise, explicit, and public. The Japanese has a different concept of loyalty, and openness.

5. Feedback is usually ill-timed in the United States. The feedback occurs after an event. The Japanese use group pressure to assure that performance is maintained.

6. Vagueness is a stock in trade of the Japanese, while the American tries to be explicit.

7. Understanding of self in the United States means that each individual seeks a separate meaning for his life. In Japan the communal relationship is the expression of self.

We could summarize this discussion by listing a few attributes that would improve American business practice:

1. Train executives in technology rather than business.

2. Learn to learn from others. America has the NIH (Not Invented Here) syndrome.

3. Expand continuing education for employers and employees.

4. Support the basic research of the industry upon which new ideas will develop.

5. Develop academic-industry cooperation.

6. Develop collaborative ventures.

These few examples indicate clearly that managers must become acquainted with international business and understand the foibles of other international traders as they expect foreigners to understand them. The old cliché that we live in one world is truer each day.

The executive is under great pressure. When Nissan can reduce total cost of an automobile up to 20 percent by changing work hours and reducing the costs of parts, it behooves the American CEO to look behind to see who is catching up. To be trained as an American manager is now a stigma rather than a mark of prestige because, as Lester Thurow has said, "American managers are now trained for a world that is no longer there. The executive must realize he/she is now living in a technical and global economy and adjust his thinking towards this end. If he/she does not, the situation cannot improve."[19]   Failure to observe these ideas may serve to explain the rapid turnover of managers in industry and elsewhere.

SORRY, YOU'RE FIRED

Many executives are facing the threat of change in their lifestyles.[20] The change may take several directions. One is discharge. The other is demotion. Either may be preceded by a series of steps that are easily recognized. The modern executive may face this rocky road under present economic circumstances. AT&T cut 35,000 white-collar workers by 1988 and Monsanto has dropped almost 7,000 workers. All in all about 500,000 white-collar middle, and upper-echelon executives will be fired by the end of 1990. Other companies such as IBM have not laid off many workers but have encouraged early retirement among the upper group. The group that had expected to sail under fair winds into retirement is finding rough seas and storm signals in every direction. Yet reduction of executives is good for the company. When AT&T reduced the executive staff by 20 percent the profits rose by 41 percent. Clearly idlers were discovered and dismissed.

Of greater concern is the set-in-the-mold attitude of many upper executives. Studies have found that many have been in the same line of work for twenty or more years and are unable to change or adapt to new ways that would make then more marketable. In fact, the results are clearly demonstrated by the fact the reemployment rates of senior executives have actually dropped while other groups have increased. The job structure of executives is a pyramid, and it is difficult to force one's way into the top at a late age.

And the losers are not the only sufferers. The winners also suffer. Those who survive the ousters find a guilt about performance mixed with fear about the future and this does not lead to increased productivity. The fear is not very realistic since most companies have found a quick bloodletting rather than a prolonged hemorrhage is better for the company. Those who survive the first onslaught are likely to continue to survive. But reeducation is necessary.

PRODUCTIVITY IN THE WHITE COLLAR WORKER

There are some steps that could be taken to improve productivity. Some are major procedures that are anathema to the white-collar workers, but may some-day be necessary:

1. Reduce the number of steps in the hierarchy to four or five by laying off 50 percent of the administrative staffs.

2. Reduce perks.

3. Pay only on achievement.

4. Equip executives with word processors and computers and require them to do their own work.

5. Reduce accounting demands to actual needs (accounting is a defensive measure and much is not necessary to run a business).

6. Find new sources of growth in industry.

7. Examine the capital-labor ratio. At one time it was less expensive to substitute machines (capital) for labor but now that machines are growing more and more expensive, the reverse may be true.

A major change on the industrial management scene is the installation of a system of payment for results rather than for mere presence on the job. At one time not so long ago, the executive moved up the ladder with regular pay raises. Time was on his side. Now some 33 percent of all contracts include bonuses for work rather than guaranteed raises, and in many cases the bonuses are substituted for raises.[7] This has been accompanied by a loss of perks such as the company car. Most recipients are not happy with the change. In good times when the economy is moving upward, the bonuses are likely to be high, but in depressions there may be no bonuses at all. Many Japanese companies are now feeling exactly this pinch.

From the standpoint of the company, it is an excellent way to force productivity on employees. When a bad year hit a steel company in North Carolina the CEO took a 40 percent pay cut as a result of the bonus system. On the other hand several companies not adopting the plan did poorly, but gave executive staffs a 10 percent salary raise for no apparent reason. Little wonder that the productivity of the American executive is low.

The executive must also learn that a new style of management is now in force. The authoritarian manager is now considered to be insecure. As the management consultant, Joan Iaconetti says, the new-style manager must be tough but wise, and the wise element must be foremost.[10]

The wise executive keeps one ear to the ground, the ground of his subordinates and boss. Hearing from them—or not hearing from them—may be a sign of trouble.

REFERENCES

1. B. Brophy and M. Walsh, "Thanks for the Bonus, But Where's My Raise?" *U.S. News and World Report,* July 20, 1987, p. 43.

2.   B. Brophy and M. Walsh, "The 'Just in Time' Worker," *U.S. News and World Report,* November 23, 1987, p. 45.

3.   C. Hartman and S. Pearlstein, "The Joy of Working," *INC.,* November 1987, p. 61.

4.   "Slaves of the New Machine," *Washington Post National Weekly,* January 25, 1988, p. 6.

5.   A. Bernstein, "Help Wanted," *Business Week,* August 10, 1987, p. 48.

6.   R. J. Spinrad, "Office Automation," *Science* 215:808 (1982).

7.   C. O'dell, *Major Findings from People, Performance, and Pay.* Houston, Tex.: American Productivity and Quality Center, 1986.

8.   A. Sanoff, "A Watershed in the Workplace," *U.S. News and World Report,* May 30, 1988, p. 52.

9.   T. K. Bikson and B. A. Gutek, *New Technology in the Office.* New York: Work in America Institute, 1980.

10.   "CEOs and Employees," *INC.,* November 1987, p. 70.

11.   American Productivity and Quality Center, *Positioning Corporate Staff for the Nineties.* Houston, Tex.: American Productivity and Quality Center, 1989.

12.   J. G. Ling and G. D. Wallace, "Government-to-Industry Technology Transfer," *Bridge* 19 (3):21 (Fall 1989).

13.   C. A. Zraket, "Dual-Use Technologies and National Competitiveness," *Bridge* 19 (3):14 (Fall 1989).

14.   E. E. Ghiselli, *Explorations in Managerial Talent.* Pacific Palisades, Calif.: Goodyear, 1971.

15.   R. R. Blake and J. S. Mouton, *The Managerial Grid.* Houston, Tex.: Gulf Publishing, 1964.

16.   F. E. Fiedler and M. M. Chelmers, *Leadership and Effective Management.* Glenview, Ill.: Scott, Foresman, 1974.

17.   T. Moore, "Personality Tests Are Back," *Fortune,* March 30, 1987, p. 74.

18.   R. M. Kanter, *Men and Women of the Corporation.* New York: Basic Books, 1977.

19.   L. Thurow, *The Zero-Sum Society.* New York: Basic Books, 1980.

20.   B. Brophy and M. Walsh, "You're Fired," *U.S. News and World Report,* March 23, 1987, p. 50.

8
Quality—An Educational Goal

America faces a serious dilemma. The quality of our products has not increased with costs or in competition with better quality overseas. The evidence is clear and indisputable. The average Japanese car has six defects as compared to the one hundred in the average American car as it comes off the assembly line. In addition, the average American car requires 4 repairs per year to the Japanese car's one trip to the repair shop. When the Japanese took over the television manufacturing operation of Motorola in this country they reduced defects in sets from 150 per thousand to 4 per thousand within five months. The Japanese point out the problem is that 80 percent of the defects are due to the failure of manufacturers to build things right in the first place. The emphasis in Japan is upon quality while in the United States it has failed to become the bottom line as the CEOs tend more and more to be financial rather than manufacturing experts. We have not yet learned that prevention is better than treatment in medicine and in manufacturing. We have pointed out earlier that the American corporation is not concerned with the manufacturing of products but with the merger, acquisition, and money management that will return a greater profit to the company. The United States leads the world in innovative ideas but lags far behind most of it in applying the innovation to the world of industry. [1]

Executives have not insisted upon quality. It is their responsibility, but it has largely been evaded. The resistance of the American car manufacturers to introducing new safety measures is a case in point. The failure of a company to admit to the poor placement of exhausts leading to fires in several cars with reported deaths led the company not to improve quality, but to fight suits for damages despite the fact that Ralph Nader had pointed out the defect many times. Supervision is the hallmark of quality and excellence and has not been defined well in the United States. The lack of supervision and its effect on quality is apparent when it is considered that the average worker is paid more than 7 percent of his/her salary for hours he/she does not work. [2] The rampant cheating in the school systems that extended to the prestigious service academies is another example of poor supervision. The failure to instill values into the workers or students is also a mark of poor supervision and lack of quality.

The failure to demand quality in work is compounded by poor production methods. W.E. Deming, who started the revolution in quality in Japan, has stated that from 15 to 40 percent of the cost of any American article represents waste in manufacture. When Ford appreciated this fact and employed Deming to restructure their operations, they rapidly became the leading American car producer with the slogan "Quality is job 1." Yet Ford has recently recalled 15,000 Econovan ambulances to repair serious defects, indicating the system is not perfect.

Yet there are outstanding examples in the United States of companies that were forced to meet competition and did so by improving quality. Xerox for many years had control of the market for copiers. Then Japan entered the competition and began to undercut prices and produce machines with better quality. Xerox was forced to embark upon a program of quality control. They rapidly improved quality from 10,000 defective items/million to 920 per million in six years with a reduction of 10,000 in the work force. They plan to repeat the same improvement in quality over the next ten years. General Electric, faced with the same problem, introduced a new electronic surveillance system for the assembly line so that it became impossible to make more than two defective parts in a row because the electronic system halted production when two defective parts came through the line and were rejected. The assembly line now makes an air-conditioning compressor every five seconds with only 900 employees.[1]   United Motors in Fremont, California, adopted the Japanese system with cooperation from a Japanese car manufacturer. Job classifications were reduced to four, just-in-time inventory was adopted, the Kaizen (search for improvement) method was introduced, and quality control was expanded. Within a few years they were producing the two top-rated cars (Toyota in Japan, and Nova in the United States).

Harley Davidson was losing its entire market to the Japanese motorcycle. It introduced new methods, increased productivity by 45 percent, increased quality greatly, and recaptured 50 percent of the market. These are a few examples of what management can accomplish when the goal is clearly focused on quality.

In each case, the company was willing to take new ideas and introduce them step by step into the operations as a reduction of theory to practice. The Japanese have always been masters of this technique. The best example is the computer chip. In the beginning, one transistor or component was placed on a chip. Now, by slow incremental steps, we see one million transistors on a single chip. And in the same period of time the cost per transistor has decreased markedly. A major reason for the large price decrease has been quality control. The ability to make chips that do not have to be discarded for bad circuitry, and as a result the development of manufacturing technology leading to the production of large-scale integrated circuits has brought the Japanese to a lead in the field.

The Ministry for International Trade and Industry (MITI) of Japan has estimated that at present the Japanese are ahead of the Americans in memory devices, VCRs, PBXs, printers, robots, and ceramics. The Americans lead Japan in only one area of major technology—database technology. [3]

Another case in point where the United States has lagged behind other countries is in the production of nuclear power. We have had plant breakdowns, cost overruns of 300 percent, and frequent shutdown of operations for faulty procedures. Great Britain, on the other hand, has found nuclear energy is so cheap it will require a reduction of 20 percent in the price of coal to make it competitive with nuclear power. France draws 40 percent of its energy from nuclear reactors and Japan is rapidly approaching this level. No other country has had the problems in production, costs, or energy shutdowns of the United States, excluding the meltdown of an outdated plant at Chernobyl in the Soviet Union. The United States cannot produce nuclear energy to compete with other forms of energy, plants are produced with poor quality, and the time of construction is too long. France requires about six years from design to operation of a nuclear plant while the United States requires twelve years. One may argue that this is the result of overzealous government regulation and there is some truth in the statement. However, the reverse may be true. Poor quality of construction may have required more regulation. And certainly the United States has had more trouble with plant failures than other countries.[1]

We could continue this litany of disaster indefinitely. However, a few more examples will suffice to illustrate the difference between quality-conscious workers and workers who are interested in dollars. Hewlett-Packard found that American-made computer chips had nineteen times the rate of failure of Japanese chips. Products of all kinds were recalled from the American market 19 million times in 1978. One tire manufacturer was forced to spend $182 million to recall and replace poorly made tires. One of the most damning statements about American industry came from the Martin company, which investigated low quality in some of its products. The company found that poor quality was accepted as a norm by the workers because the managers had not emphasized that quality was *expected* of all workers.

American CEOs do not realize that quality is reflected in the bottom line. Germany spends about three times as much of the sales price as the United States on quality control, and this is reflected in the quality of the product. But there is more. Quality in manufacturing saves costs in the long run. It is cheaper to manufacture well than to repair goods that have to be returned. The high rate of return of new American automobiles for repair of defects in manufacture is a case in point. It has been estimated it will cost $0.03 to correct a defect at the plant, $3.00 to correct it in subassembly, and $30.00 to correct it in service after the product is made. Hewlett-Packard has estimated that it costs more to repair a unit in the field due to poor quality production than the unit costs in the first place. And the money invested in quality control is returned many fold. Fewer rejects leads to better output and therefore more profits. It may be hoped the automobile industry is beginning to realize this basic fact. Despite the fact that warranties have been extended, *Consumer Reports* finds the average American car still has many more defects than the Japanese automobile when delivered to the showroom. American manufacturers have resorted to the establishment of extended service departments in auto dealers (Mr. Goodwrench) in order to allay the public concern about the numerous defects in American cars. This is a poor solution to concern for quality in the assembly of the automobile in the first place. In a rapidly developing industry technology is developed in order to support better productivity which in turn creates a beneficial cycle where the increased productivity produces new profits that can be plowed back into development, and so the cycle continues. In the United States the additional funds are used for acquisitions of business and very little is invested in the future of the company, which is a shortsighted approach to the problem. Many Japanese companies have a ten-to-twenty-year plan of development while most American companies have almost no future plans beyond the next year and the dividends that will be paid. Quality is measured by the size of the return on investment. Quality or the lack of it is in the eye of the beholder.

The American health care system is said to be the best in the world from the standpoint of actual tests performed and treatments conducted. From the standpoint of cost, service to all members of society, infant mortality, and other parameters, it ranks lower than most other developed nations. Furthermore, the quality of service rendered, although high, is tempered by too many surgeries, overuse of drugs, and long hospital stays. Technology is excellent but it is overused. There is no evidence, for example, that helicopter service for the injured saves lives, but the cost may run as high as $100,000 per patient. A later chapter will explore health care in detail.

As measured by output in tons of grain or in production per acre, the American farmer outproduces the world. However, this is bought at a dear price and raises the question of excellence. In the old days, a farmer and a mule used an amount of energy to produce an equivalent amount of food. Now one calorie of food energy requires almost one hundred calories of energy to produce. The profligate use of energy for machinery, for transportation, and for packaging may exhaust the energy supply before we exhaust the land. A few cents' worth of grain in a breakfast food requires enormous resources and energy to produce the package that may cost more than the contents.

And we are exhausting the land. Each additional output of grain energy now requires an additional 20 percent more fertilizer than a few years ago. The depletion of the land is further aggravated by the use of water for irrigation which washes the salts into the soil and renders it infertile. Water costs less for the farmer than any other resource when it should cost more. Reisner has pointed out that water has been diverted for purposes that are improvident.[4] For example, a switch in water use from pasture to orange groves, and to vegetable farming from cattle raising, would save crucial water supplies for other uses.

Education is also an industry where quality and excellence are often confused. We have a good educational system starting at the college level as is clearly demonstrated by the large numbers of foreign students who come to the United

States for higher education. Yet quality and the innovation going with it have not been exploited by industry. We have pointed out the long lag time between invention and development in the United States as compared to other countries and this may be a fault of education. We must do better.

WHAT IS QUALITY?

Quality is a standard of performance that will produce the desired product. It is a measure of excellence and may be determined in several ways:

1. *Transcendental quality* is the highest possible standard and produces outputs that are the finest possible.

2. *Product quality* is a standard set by the industry and may be variable depending upon costs and other factors. An excellent example is the determination not to use air bags for protection in cars although they obviously save lives.

3. *User quality* is the quality demanded by the consumer that may be less than optimum. Consumer demand for quality is increasing as the result of import of high-quality goods and may raise standards of the industry.

4. *Manufacturing quality* is the conformance to specifications that may be good or bad. The quality is essentially based upon the idea that every piece produced on a production line should be like every other piece.

5. *Value-based quality* is the quality barely necessary to return a profit or sell the product.

It is apparent that each of these is somewhat dependent upon the others. Refrigerators produced in a production line may be exactly like all others, or every student may be able to pass a standardized test, but if this quality does not satisfy demand, further refinement of the standard may be necessary. By the same token, each of these represents a totally different approach to the product and may result in vastly different qualities. If we look at quality from another standpoint, we find it is based on performance, features, reliability, conformance to standards, durability, serviceability, esthetics, and perceived quality by the consumer.

Every industry decides upon the quality standard it will emphasize. The Japanese have emphasized reliability and conformance to standards; banks have adopted service as the quality standard; Steinway Piano Company has used esthetics as a measure of quality; and many American manufacturers have adopted the perceived quality by the consumer as a standard. Automotive makers, for example, have played upon the American taste for the flashy and the big in cars without due consideration of performance. This is clearly demonstrated by a survey of manufacturers. Some 65 percent thought the consumer could identify quality and would demand it and they thought their product fulfilled the requirements, but surveys of consumers revealed only 16 percent had an idea about quality and the purchase was based on other factors.

It is possible that the consumer is rising to the quality call. The influx of high-quality goods from the Orient and Europe has focused attention on quality as a part of any purchase, clearly demonstrated by the increasing purchases of Japanese cars. Mallory, writing in the *Wall Street Journal,* has argued that CEOs must choose between quality and the fast buck if they are to survive foreign competition. This places the CEO in an unenviable position. Surveys of investors clearly indicate that they are not interested in quality but in the return on investment. A sales job must be done on investors to convince them that profits will be greater in the future if funds are invested in quality control now. However, it is not clear that CEOs believe this and until they do, the share of the world market held by the United States will continue to decrease.

Identical statements could be made for other sectors of the society. In medical care, we have not defined for the administrator or the physician the standard of good care. Is it the care rendered by the specialist to the individual patient or is it the prevention of disease, the treatment of all the population equally, or the demonstration of a cost benefit of any treatment? In education we have not set goals of achievement and selected teachers who are competent to meet those goals. One attempt to clearly define goals for education has been made by Prince George's County, Maryland, which issues an "Educational Warrant" to every student who graduates and has fulfilled all academic requirements. Students are warranted to be able to hold a job and perform the required task or the school system will retrain them free of charge.

The effects of industrial efforts including agriculture have not been assessed for impact on the environment. We have assumed that rural America is pristine and do not take into account the effects of pesticides, improper water use, and other poor practices.

American industry as a whole has fought any environmental controls for the protection of the North Slope, forest destruction in the West, acid rain in the Northeast, taconite mining around the Great Lakes, and automobile pollution in large cities. The cities themselves have fought against regulations to improve the environment. We are now looking at a future including global warming with attendant disturbances in agriculture, destruction of the ozone layers with increasing cancer as a result, and other hazards of which we now know nothing. All could be controlled by industry, albeit at great cost. Should we save industry and destroy the world?

We will end this discussion by raising a serious question. Is there a social contract between the consumer and the producer? If there is, who decides quality? The government has taken the position that such a contract does exist, and the producer is required to make a safe and useful product. Is it also required to make a quality product? And who defines the quality, the consumer or the producer?

The above suggests that we must redefine the engineering profession to think in terms of the many facets involved in relatively simple decisions about production. Engineers bring to the decision-making process a sense of priority and allocation of resources that may make them a dominant influence in the future. However, as S. Ramo has pointed out, engineering schools do not usually offer courses in engineering technology, business leaders are scientifically illiterate, and innovation and technology are separated from each other.

The Japanese are developing quality control in new ways by using artificial intelligence (AI) to make reasonable decisions. AI techniques permit a host of intelligent decisions. A system using the decision-making power of AI can decide upon knowledge to make a decision, interpret the data base, diagnose trouble, monitor processes, predict future actions, learn assumptions to make decisions, and help plan operations. There is a tendency in the United States to choose the acceptable but not the best performance. AI permits the best performance consistent with all parameters. The use of this technique has led to the development of a socially integrated technology defining cognitive procedures, distributing work, and dividing responsibility.

A. Matsumoto, writing on Japanese management in the 1982 issue of *Journal of Japanese Trade and Industry,* has remarked that quality can be produced only by encouraging employee development and upward progression, by allowing the employees to set standards of work, welcoming and implementing employee suggestions, to allow executives and employees to learn from each other, and allowing the worker to supervise the production process. We implement very few of these quality control measures inbred into the Japanese economy.

S. Ishihara, a Japanese industrialist, has recently angered the American business community by writing a book that could be subtitled 'The U.S.—A Nation of Crybabies' but is actually entitled *The Japan that Can Say NO.* [5] He points out that one of the major problems of quality is the American CEO who does not deal in quality but in money games requiring little R and D and product development, requires quarterly reports of increasing profits, makes no long-term plans, fails to think about the good of the company as opposed to the individual good, and fails to have a "people" orientation toward the worker. As a result, our mistakes, our loss of markets, and our import-export imbalance are all our own fault.

There are some indications that American industry has realized its fault and is making some changes. *U.S. News and World Report* for September 17, 1990, reported that the number of firms operating in only one industry has increased from about 15 percent to 25 percent in five years, that those operating in twenty or more industries has decreased 50 percent, and factory output per hour has increased dramatically. All of these are excellent signs that some changes are coming. Unfortunately, much of the change has been attributed to spinoffs, mergers, and buyouts, which reduced the number of diversified companies and thus improved quality.

REFERENCES

1.   "Responding to the Competitive Challenge: The Technological Dimension," *Bridge* 18 (1):3 (Spring 1988).

2.   M. N. Baily, "Productivity in a Changing World," *Brookings Institution* 18:1 (1981).

3.   E. A. Torrero, "R and D," *IEEE Spectrum* 27 (10), entire issue (October 1990).

4.   M. Reisner, "The Next Water War," *Issues in Science and Technology* 5 (2): 98 (Winter 1988–89).

5.   S. Ishihara, *The Japan That Can Say No.* New York: Simon and Schuster, 1991.

9

Planning for Innovation

Management is in many respects similar in all industries. Budgets must be prepared and implemented, communications must be established, day-to-day operations must be attended to, and long-range goals must be defined. The way the executive goes about achieving these aims results in either excellence or in a poorer quality of management. Many aspects of the process combine to determine the overall effects of management practice on success. And the ability to innovate offers the best chance.

All business trends must begin with planning. Whether in government, academia or industry, planning is a three-step process and all three steps must be in place before an adequate system is functional. The first step is *strategic* planning where broad general objectives are laid down. The strategy must be in some sort of quantitative and qualitative terms so that a budget can later be formulated. Once the objectives or goals have been set, *tactical* planning takes the information and produces specific measures to implement it. These measures are in a broad context of location, method, and evaluation. Finally the tactical plans are handed to the *operational* planner, who devises the day-by-day, step-by-step means of accomplishing the goals.

An example may clear the air. A strategic goal might be to produce 10 million cars in 1996. The tactical goals would identify the goals (kind of cars), the methods (degree of automation, design), the political barriers, and many other details. The operational personnel would see to space, personnel, equipment, and delivery of raw materials.

This logical progression of achievement has not been common in health care. For example, we have launched a multibillion dollar program in heart bypass surgery without evaluation of the success of the method, without planning for how many should be operated upon, and without a review of the resources. The automobile industry launched its plan for construction of large cars just at the time gasoline prices rose and the Japanese invaded the United States with the small car. In both cases the strategy was poor.

Proper planning also implies control of the process. The strategic planning is usually conducted by upper echelons, the tactical planning by middle-level administrators, and the operational planning by division heads. At each level the participants must embrace the plan in all details and be prepared to implement it. This does not happen under the usual circumstances. Each level of management has its own objectives that may not coincide with the level above. Thus every manager must make it a point to know the objectives of reporting employees.

The necessary information is different at each level of planning. The strategic planner requires general information about the locality, the politics, and the community. The tactical planner must know about resource allocation and the source of funds in both external and internal sources, while the operational planner is concerned with the day-to-day internal operations. The time spans are also different. The strategic planner is concerned with years of effort, the tactical planner with shorter time spans, while the operational planner is concerned with day-to-day operations.

Planning without evaluation of the results is a waste of time. Evaluation is a three-step operation. Objectives can be evaluated on the basis of *structure* a measure of whether the resources to accomplish the desired objective are available. Are plants built and personnel trained? The evaluation of *process* determines whether the units are functioning properly. Does an assembly line flow smoothly, are materials delivered on time? The highest stage of evaluation is *outcome*. What was the actual productivity?

The American consumer would do well to examine these steps in light of present knowledge. The health care system, for example, is based solely upon process planning. Is an operation done in the most efficient manner? Does a patient stay in the hospital longer than necessary? There is no attempt to measure outcomes. Is the patient better after the procedure? Was the result worth the cost? Has quality of life improved six months after treatment? We will examine some of these questions in a later chapter.

A discussion of objectives and evaluation would mean little without some sort of standards against which results can be judged. As a general rule there are two type of standards: standards of quality and standards of quantity. Standards of quality measure the attributes defining the goals of performance. Standards of quantity usually refer to the ability to mass produce a given product. We must consider both kinds of evaluation if a product is to measure up to the desires of the consumer. In order to achieve uniformity in standards, the authority to fix limits is usually delegated to some organization with the expertise and the pervasiveness to establish standards and to enforce control over the performance to achieve the set limits. Almost all specialized organizations from the National Association of Manufacturers to the American Medical Association regulate quality in some fashion and exercise control over output and performance. However, such organizations tend to enforce limits on themselves that are the lowest common denominator of quality adhered to by all members. The ultimate arbitrater may be the general public setting its own acceptable standards or refusing to purchase poorer goods. In situations such as environmental control or purity of drugs, the government may intervene to set standards.

Standards are useful in themselves because they help to set quality. A standard allows coordination of effort between producers of like products and allows the consumer to judge between two producers. A major advantage in having standards of quantity is for mass production. Every piece is produced in a like manner, but nothing is said about quality. If the standards are set high enough, both quantity and quality can be achieved, but such is not always the case. The Japanese have a reputation for building fine cars meeting both production and quality standards while American manufacturers have met quantity standards but have apparently fallen short in quality standards.

It is unfortunate that in many cases we do not have the knowledge to set adequate standards. What should be the standards for auto emissions? What are the standards to prevent acid rain?

Organizations tend to become rigid as they adopt standards and then they resist change. When an assembly line has been set up, whether it is for cars or students, the process becomes fixed and hard to change. Change requires a series of steps including recognition that a problem exists, diagnosis, identification of an alternate strategy, determination of methods to implement change, implementation, and evaluation of the results. All too often industry becomes complacent with the status quo and change is resisted from the top down. The sudden decision of the Ford company to produce a European-style car while General Motors continued to produce the older style look-alikes is a case in point. The results were obvious. Ford gained a major share of the market. This discourse has focused on the methods used by organizations. The theme could be extended indefinitely and can be found in all standard textbooks on management.[1] However, it is the manager who observes the planning and implementation process and creates excellence from it.

Adams in his perceptive book *Conceptual Blockbusting* has suggested that the basic problems of managers fall in several classes:[2]

1. Defining the problem too closely—seeing the trees but not the forest.
2. Isolating the specific problem needing priority attention.
3. Inability to see more than one way to solve the problem.
4. Seeing what is expected rather than attempting to find the unusual.
5. Saturation of the mind with masses of data of varying importance.

There is little need to comment on these criteria—they are self-evident. The United States is noted for invention. The bulk of all inventions, including most of the great ones, were made in the United States. This is now changing and more patents are filed from Germany and Japan than from the United States. An invention is of little value unless it is exploited, and the innovation of the American manager is notably shortsighted. The United States may win the invention race but lose on productivity. In addition, there is no spirit of innovation. A new product is invented and then produced, but that is the end. Next year there is no marked improvement in a cyclic process that should result in better production, better innovation, and better products in an endless cycle. The Americans have not learned this trick, or another the Japanese developed years ago, the ability to effect a quick turnaround. It has been said with some justification that when the Americans invent something, the companies argue about production, while the Japanese are selling it the day after tomorrow and selling a better product the next week. The company with the quicker cycle is the winner. The only way to affect the cycle is to affect the people who control it, the managers. The long time required for the car industry to turn around from the production of large cars to smaller models has almost allowed the Japanese to corner the market for small cars.

Adams goes on to point out that most executives suffer from taboos in problem solving: the thought that money can solve all problems, that the scientific approach will solve all problems, and that intuitive reasoning and hunches are bad while reason, logic, and numbers are good. He makes a point of Arthur Koestler's statement that the real inspiration is the ability to combine previously unrelated structures in such a way that more can be obtained from the combination than from the sum of all of the inputs together.[3] But it is intuition that provides the insights to use different input materials to arrive at a new solution.

The American executive suffers from a malady characterized by fear of mistakes, inability to tolerate ambiguity, failure to think long enough about a problem before decision, excessive zeal, and lack of imagination. The Japanese executive does not have the same problems, but his problems revolve around peer and group pressure, fear of failure, and loss of face.

These statements imply that both the American and Japanese executives suffer from a lack of creativity. Creativity occurs in several forms. The process of innovation takes many ideas and rearranges them into a new concept. Creation can also occur by synthesis where ideas are blended together to improve the present situation. Creation may be accomplished by extension, where an idea in use is extended to a new use or method. Some writers have listed duplication as a form of creativity but these writers disagree. In addition to the formation of new ideas from a series of older concepts, there is a form of innovation arising a priori as a result of a sudden flight of intuition such as Einstein's theory of relativity.

Creativity is a good thing, and all corporations try to develop and encourage it. This is the reason most companies that can afford it maintain research departments. In addition, many companies try to stimulate creativity in their employees. General Electric, for example, identifies a desirable output and then encourages researchers to develop any kind of input leading to the end result. The

California Institute of Technology developed a grid structure on which inputs, outputs, and constraints are plotted in an attempt to stimulate thought. A.D. Little has attempted to teach creativity in groups by dividing the process into three periods: a period during which a problem is presented and analyzed, a period of generalization where the problem is examined by a group, and finally a period of synthesis or model building where a resolution is attempted. Others have adopted the Delphi Technique in which a group is presented with a problem and each member is asked for a solution. The solutions are listed, and the members are asked to choose among them. Finally a consensus is reached. This may not be true innovation because much of the reasoning may be from known facts that are simply manipulated.

The manager who would be an innovator must learn to examine problems with new eyes, isolate the problem and determine its parameters, broaden the basic problem into as many areas as possible, define the conditions to be obtained on solution, and seek as many solutions as possible so a choice can be made. Kenneth Boulding, the science philosopher, has pointed out that the process of creativity involves the determination of an internal truism or internal logic base.[4] It may be based in mathematics, the classification of the information into identifiable sectors, the development of empiricism, or a perception of need. The connectivity to other ideas or processes may involve statistics, and finally the output or results. Insights follow most of these steps, although some few individuals, Albert Einstein, Isaac Newton, and others, appear to have had a flash of genius allowing leaps of understanding, and these may not require internal logic or truism as they invent the truism as they proceed. It is interesting that this theory does not imagine science for science's sake, but rather a process resulting in something definable.

INNOVATION

One of the criteria for excellence is continuous advancement in an area of expertise. And the development of expertise implies training and education. Although Ed Land could develop Polaroid without a degree, and Thomas Edison created 1,000 inventions with a grammar school education, this is not the norm. The rapid rise of technology demands greater attention to education and to the nurturing of innovation.[3] Only by invention, development, and technological advancement can a country stay viable. To meet competition and retain a world market requires maintaining an active research and development effort aimed at outperforming the competition and opening new areas for development and trade. The American CEO is responsible for not developing innovative procedures. The fault lies in the CEO and his previous training, and in the correct use of the work force.

There is great concern about the lack of innovation in companies, particularly in the large companies. While it is true more innovation is needed in the emerging areas and in the small companies and less is required in the developed production areas, it is unfortunate that larger companies have become stultified and innovation is now found largely in the companies with under $10 million in business sales. As Ramo has pointed out, real innovations do not usually come from larger companies.[5] He cites the transportation industry that did not develop the airplane, energy companies that did not develop electricity, or adding machine companies that ignored the computer, although each had the base to make the innovations. New companies and some new people were required to initiate the changes. The Massachusetts Institute of Technology with a worldwide reputation for innovation has a practice of spinning off small companies with each invention of its faculty that has industrial promise. The practice has paid off in income for the university, and some 85 successful companies have resulted.

THE BUREAUCRACY

A major problem occurring in all industry worldwide, but apparently more predominant in American companies, is the creation of an entrenched bureaucracy that hampers innovation.[6] The bureaucracy in the large organization has the same effect on innovation and new ideas as does the bureaucracy in the federal government, and with the same overall effect. In his excellent study, *Inside Bureaucracy*, A. Downs has written that as an organization grows, the upper echelons become set in their ways, stultified, and without new ideas. The bureaucracy becomes self-perpetuating.

In the beginning a bureaucracy is a fine idea. It permits organization to exist, channels directions of effort, and develops rules of operation. But, as Parkinson has remarked, when an organization reaches a staff size of about 1,000 personnel, it becomes internally self-perpetuating.[7] The large number of individuals means that paperwork can be shuffled from desk to desk without the need for any outside influence. As the bureaucracy increases in size, the number of "idlers," those individuals who are now outside the normal pathway of communications and contribute nothing to the company, also increases. The reasons are embedded in the bureaucracy itself where there is a real fear of disbanding old operations. As a result new methods or branches are appended to the old, and the number of idlers grows. This has been clearly demonstrated in several recent developments. The very fact that a company can reduce its executive staff by 40 percent with an actual increase in productivity is a clear indication of the number of idlers in a large corporation.[8] Stultification is clearly seen in the steel industry where a reluctance to abandon the old steel-making processes in favor of the new continuous method has resulted in the demise of several of the largest steel companies in the country. The present estimates are that Taiwan, Korea, and Japan produce steel at about $70 per ton less than the United States.

In direct contrast, the new and smaller steel companies in this country that have not yet had time to build bureaucracy have developed new processing methods and have taken over the steel industry. Most steel is now made in small plants in many locations. The failure of Detroit to recognize changes in automobile style and design is another case in point. Only when Ford obtained a new CEO who was willing to clean out the bureaucracy was Ford able to dominate the market through innovation of new models for the first time in decades.[8]

Another very serious problem arises with the aging bureaucracy. As the young zealots who formed the organization see regimentation and routine take over, they depart, leaving behind the mediocre managers whose only desire is to maintain the status quo. This situation creates more idlers, and the organization goes downhill. The result is an organization immune to new ideas, hidebound in rules of operation, and occupied by older bureaucrats who maintain their positions at all costs. At this point, the only solution is to remove the upper echelons and replace them with a new crew. Obviously, this will be opposed strenuously by those in power. The one fortunate result of the takeover binge on Wall Street is the wholesale removal of echelons of power structure of the deceased companies. The collapse of the large number of savings and loan companies with the resulting removal of tiers of executives, high-priced, and often incompetent, may well increase productivity of the banking industry.

INNOVATION AND TECHNOLOGY

Another problem for the organization lies in the rise of technology.[9] Many old-line managers do not understand new technology, and as a result fear it. In contrast to the Japanese, most American managers are business majors, adding to the fear of technology. This is also clearly seen in the medical complex where most physicians have refused to use personal computers despite their obvious advantages.

On the other hand, automation is clearly the wave of the future, and many companies have dived into the field to automate processes that can be done more cheaply and perhaps better by human hands. The Japanese have recognized this problem and the robots in their plants have replaced personnel only where it is clearly a cost benefit to do so and where the decision has been made by the workers who are asked to devise the automation and have the training to do it.[5] There is considerable question as to whether some technology is designed to forward the image of the company rather than the needs and ends of society.

Lewis Thomas, president of Sloan-Kettering Cancer Institute, has pointed out that in science there are three identities. *Bad science* which does not solve any problems, and for example, in medicine does not produce anything except income for the physician. In industry, research on the production of tobacco which may damage health although it returns a healthy profit, is a good example. *Halfway* science is a partial solution to problems and in medicine is exemplified by the heart lung operations, transplants, or bypass surgery; or the half way standards of the auto industry in controlling emissions that ameliorate the problems of pollution of the atmosphere but do not solve them. Finally, there is *true* science which solves the problem. In medicine this is usually the preventive measures that are low cost, high benefit solutions to problems such as AIDS antibody development, mammography, and some computerized axial tomography (CAT) scans and the development of procedures such as the lithotripter that dissolves kidney stones, thus preventing costly operative procedures. In industry it may be that safer transportation requires designing roads for safety instead of designing the car at great expense to protect the driver as we now do.

The innovative solutions to many problems are not always readily apparent, but it is essential that industry make every effort to expand innovative talent and encourage it even when it appears to be disruptive to the general operation. The fact that the Japanese worker makes many suggestions each year and most are accepted by management suggests that innovative talent lies in many directions.

Automobile companies have spent millions of dollars attempting to evade governmental requirements for pollution emissions, gasoline mileage, and safety. Their designs have been oriented toward evading the regulatory needs rather than fulfilling the consumer desire and attempting to meet standards. This is poor technology, poorly applied, and it illustrates clearly a resistance to excellence.[5] Again, innovation may be the solution to the problem. The Swedes have built a model car which obtains more than one hundred miles to the gallon, does not use gasoline as fuel, and is almost nonpolluting, but it has not been adopted because of the public antipathy to small cars, another bar to innovation.

Innovation is the proper answer to poor technology. However, for innovation to be successful we must carefully distinguish between the new versus a modification of an old process, radical changes versus incremental changes, and science versus engineering.[10] American managers have been deficient in all of these. The failure to adopt the front-wheel-drive automobile despite the clear superiority demonstrated in European models is a case in point. The quick fix rather than the new idea has been the method adopted by American manufacturers in designing automobile engines and steel mills, in the old time-worn style, while other countries have proceeded along a path of innovation with rotary engines and continuous casting processes. Even the Z-idea of corporation management originated in the United States, was exploited by the Japanese, and is now being imported back into the country as a completely new idea.

We have looked at the problem of creativity from the positive side. There is also a negative side in the failure of managers to develop creativity. It includes:

1. Emphasis on security; the "better be safe than sorry" syndrome.
2. Putting harmony first; the "one rotten apple spoils the barrel" syndrome.
3. Substitution of routine for thinking; the "don't tell me about it just do it" syndrome.
4. Scheduling in place of "just-in-time" operations: the "this is Monday so it must be Rome" syndrome.

5. The need to demonstrate power and status over close association with personnel; the "twentieth floor" syndrome.

6. Overemphasis on order.

7. Need for firm conclusions in place of the use of innovative ideas.

In addition, many problems are difficult to solve. The researcher or the creative genius in the office may be difficult to live with, but must be tolerated if innovation is to be encouraged. This individual may be the innovator.

The ability to recognize that a failure is not the end of the world is essential if innovation is to succeed because failures are common. The determination to keep the organization flexible, awake, and discontented may be very helpful in starting new developments.

There is no question but that the United States has developed creativity and innovation to a high peak and undoubtedly leads the world in inventive genius, although other countries now show signs of catching up. Still, we have not applied the principles for innovation outlined above. Only recently, under pressure from the Japanese, have car makers decided to place a long-term warranty on automobiles. But the standards of quality are still not high and must be improved. *Consumer Reports* still finds many defects in recent models, indicating that we have not taken the crucial steps from innovation to production on the factory floor.

Our educational system lags behind the rest of the world, and the creativity we sorely need in this sector seems to be entirely missing. Unfortunately, most of the schemes for improving teaching have not dealt with subject matter but with procedure, and there is no wonder students make low SAT scores and cannot read or write well. The development of a strategy in education is no different than it is in the business world. We could also mention that the same tactics should apply to government. We have no policy of defense, health care, or education.

We may sum up the discussion by saying that all organizations must develop an attitude of creativity and encourage it in employees. The ability to recognize innovation is critical to the forward progress of any organization. And if the innovation is coupled with a plan for development of technology, for establishment of standards of manufacture or procedures, and if we observe the simple concept of determining the objective of any action and aiming for solutions to problems rather than the procedural tasks characterizing today's activity of education, government, and industry, we may yet win.

REFERENCES

1.   E. E. Ghiselli, *Explorations in Managerial Talent*. Pacific Palisades, Calif.: Goodyear, 1971.

2.   J. L. Adams, *Conceptual Blockbusting*. San Francisco: W. H. Freeman, 1974.

3.   A. Koestler, *The Ghost in the Machine.* New York: Macmillan, 1968.

4.   K. Boulding, *Conflict and Defense.* New York: Harper and Row, 1962.

5.   "Responding to the Competitive Challenge: The Technological Dimension," *Bridge* 18 (1):3 (Spring 1988).

6.   A. Downs, *Inside Bureaucracy.* Boston: Little, Brown, 1967.

7.   C. N. Parkinson, *Parkinson's Law.* New York: Ballantine Books, 1957.

8.   R. England, "Ford Shifts Gears," *Insight,* July 13, 1987, p. 8.

9.   F. Duchêne and G. Shepherd, *Managing Industrial Change in Western Europe.* New York: Frances Pinter, 1987.

10.   G. Porter, "Regaining Industrial Leadershp through R and D," *National Academy of Engineering Reports,* December 1987, p. 23.

10

Power—The Executive Prerogative

One of the attributes of the successful executive is the exercise of power.[1] Power can be used to create excellence or the opposite depending upon whether it is exercised for the benefit of the consumer or the manager. By one account, the inefficient manager, and therefore by definition the manager without excellence, is the one without power or without the good sense to use it properly. On the other hand power can be abused to the detriment of society. Adolf Hitler had power in large amounts and one can argue that he was efficient, if misguided, in what he did, but no one would claim power was exerted wisely.

All executives seek power because power is the hallmark of success. But care must be taken that the search for power is not allowed to become an individual matter. The picture of the big anteroom and the numerous secretaries will turn any executive head. It is like giving a loaded pistol to a child and telling him not to shoot. The would-be executive is bound to try it once, and then there is no stopping him/her.[2] The constant search for perks and the battle over the keys to the executive washroom may provide satisfaction to the final winner, but they may well decrease his usefulness to the organization. We have a classic example. The takeover of Gulf by Chevron resulted, after some six years, in a company that was still two distinct entities, each pursuing its own corporate way as each executive group fought for power. Only the consumer lost.

Power is not usually discussed in the textbooks on management. A quick reading of the standard titles shows that the information they supply does not apply to increasing the excellence of managers. Rather, each book stresses the role of the manager in increasing the productivity of the rest of the organization, usually based on increasing productivity of workers. Managers do not consider that they must increase their own productivity. A few examples will suffice.

Long discussions of Maslow, McCellan, or Herzberg, and similar theories in management textbooks, deal with motivating the workers, and not managers.[3] Any good manager can be assumed to be motivated and have reached the level where Maslow's principles of physiological needs, safety and security, social needs, and esteem no longer apply. Any manager who has not attained a level of safety and security and received esteem and respect, the ultimate goal of motivation for workers, has not been successful. New motivation, other than increased salary and perks, must be devised for the executive.

One may argue there is still room for Maslow's self-realization as the ultimate goal of motivation, but most managers have as the ultimate goal two aims, money and power, and all efforts are bent in this direction. If self-realization is the Yuppie with a new Mercedes, we have reached the American business goal.

Similarly, we could discuss such topics as motivation through group dynamics but the manager does not usually deal in groups. Although managers may face a board of directors from time to time, work is largely one on one, and when dealing in groups, the group is usually composed of other managers who are equally adept at using group theory. In fact, one of the complaints of most workers and of the consumers in large corporations is that the upper management does not communicate at all with other levels, and all groups seem to be clustered about the twentieth floor. Siu and Halberstam have both remarked on this phenomena.[1][4] The recent exposé on Wall Street, where many of the better financial firms were accused of trading illegally, brings to mind the old axiom of Lord Acton, "All power corrupts and absolute power corrupts absolutely." The ability to manipulate millions of dollars of other people's funds conveys a sense of absolute power and the result is corruption.

We must never forget that all power can be justified in some manner and is usually justified by an appeal for excellence. The invocation of motivation, progress, aggressive management, and the public good have all been used as excuses for usurpation of power in both government and business. All dictators gain power by some such appeal. Power leads to attempts to outguess the law by practices bordering on the dishonest. All attempts to blindfold the law by using evasive techniques, to placate the law by offering trades of immunity for legal action, and attempts to get around the law by using subterfuge are all legitimate business exercises, though questionable ethical pursuits. There is little need to catalog the lists of fraudulent activities in savings and loans, Wall Street activity, car dealers, and others to document the statement. Perusal of the daily papers should suffice.

One must always remember that power is essentially of two types. Political power achieves ends by pressure and manipulation and ethical power achieves ends by communication and understanding. Both may solve problems but they are mutually exclusive and a manager may elect to pursue either path but not both.

The manager must be powerful by definition. "A man who is unable to conceive a broad and bold plan, earn the respect of even his enemies, and who is clumsy in his own profession, is a hopeless amateur." Thus spoke Vladimir I. Lenin of the revolutionary seeking power. But power does not persist unless it is nurtured by the manager and used wisely. In the early days of the century, Eugene

Debs said, "The most vital power on this planet is the labor movement." At the time it was, but excessive demands have turned the movement into a fading giant. It faded because of two conflicting interests, the overall interests of the organization centered in the employee that should have been kept uppermost and were not, and the desire for power of the individual union manager that was often in opposition to the overall goals of the organization but led many labor leaders to demand more and more power. The connections of the union executives with the Mafia and other criminal organizations is a direct case in point.

As an individual manager, the seeker of power must be prepared to establish his credentials. Executives must learn to handle people, both subordinates and their superiors. Contact with superiors must be adjusted to provide the maximum return to the superior. This means that the seeker of power must be prepared to seek the advancement of the superior because this leads to the subordinate's advancement, to complement the strength of the boss with his strengths because this supports and promotes the superior, to avoid being a threat to the superior, which will undermine his own career, and to provide respect to the superior to convince him of one's own value, as well as the value of the superior to the organization. All may be opposed to excellence.

Power is information, and the manager who would attain power must have information in order to achieve it. Information is difficult to obtain in an organization. The lower echelons tend to present upper levels with information they would like to see rather than the true state of affairs. The creation of a staff to bypass the upward information flow and thus obtain additional information may also lead to the "yes" man syndrome that can be worse than information filtered from below. The manager must also join the old boy network existing in every organization even if he/she must assume a low status in the beginning. And the old boys are dedicated to maintenance of the status quo because failure to do so will result in the loss of power.

A member of the power network will command the respect and assistance of other members in the group. Hedrick Smith, in his excellent book *The Power Game,* has clearly demonstrated how this system works in the Pentagon deliberately to subvert excellence.[5] Weapon systems are defended even when it is clear they are unworkable because the power base of the individual depends upon having a large budget and controlling funds. Promotion and pay depend upon producing a working system, often by faking results of tests. The total funds spent on a project in the Pentagon determine promotion and pay for the project manager and represent real power in dealing with Congress, industry, and the military. The Congress and the state legislatures are not immune to the siren of power. The funds donated by PACs and given to state lawmakers are simply a brazen attempt to provide a power base for the giver. At one time it was possible to be elected to office with a few hundred thousand dollars, but now millions are required at the federal level and almost as much may be spent at the state level. It is difficult to justify expenditure of such funds as an altruistic exercise.

The power seeker must begin by following others toward power sources and by locating the kingmakers who control power but may not be in the apparent direct line of command. Although the chain of command is the president and the leaders of Congress in our government, many committee members wield more power in certain areas. The chairmen of the Appropriations and the Ways and Means committees of the Congress wield more power than many other public officials although they may be far down in the hierarchy of government.

As power is developed, it must be used. Failure to use power may result in the loss of it to others more willing to exert their own influence. The use of power means exercising influence to obtain one's goal. Power as it is used ranges across a wide gamut of endeavors beginning with education of the opponent and proceeding to persuasion, bribery, cajoling, threatening, damaging, to final elimination. The process usually begins at the most benign aspect and proceeds as necessary to the most powerful tools available. One may proceed directly to the less benign elements as did Saddam Hussein in Iraq, or proceed from one step to the next as did Hitler. Obviously only a czar will use the last steps but many managers resort to threats or damage of opponents to gain advantages. At least one well known manager has remarked that intimidation may work well.

Kenneth Boulding in his book *Conflict and Defense*, deals with the Richardson Process. Richardson developed a theory of conflict and resolution of conflict which can be applied to a variety of situations from the nation at war to the individual striving for power.[6] Boulding says that the power struggles in an organization can be studied with respect to the Richardson hypothesis. Any agency that can improve its position without harming itself will obviously do so, and so will the individual who can improve his position without harming others. When two agencies are striving for power, there must be an equilibrium between the two. Usually one or the other dominates unless a stalemate is achieved. The equilibrium may be made on a long-sighted or short-sighted basis and often the two are in conflict. The long-sighted equilibrium may be best for the individual and the company but the short-sighted position is an easier one to calculate and may be the one adopted. This has been clearly demonstrated in the automobile industry where the short-sighted approach has been adopted in order to compete with other manufacturers and the long-term effects have not been calculated. The arms race is another typical example. Each side expands its capability to produce more arms in response to a supposed threat from the other. A stalemate results. Exactly the same situation occurs when two individuals spar for power within an organization.

The real power broker will look for long-term solutions. The power seeker must always realize that when one party changes position, change will be forced on other parties in the transaction. The able executive will consider what the changes made to gain power will do to others in the organization, and whether the changes they make in response are inimical to his own aims. The balance of power is as important in an organization or between two individuals as it is between countries and the jockeying for position is often as complicated.

Decisions to gain power may require loss of excellence in the process because of infighting between power broker, as in recent leveraged buyouts where attainment of power far outweighed the pursuit of excellence in product or operations. American industry, in seeking a major market share of goods as a symbol of power, has sacrificed quality for quantity.

Managers gain power by several means. They may look for opportunity to take over an operation, may slowly inch their way into an organization one step at a time, may work below the surface with the bureaucracy to gain a foothold, may form coalitions with others to gain an advantage, or may avoid any confrontation and gradually establish power through expertise in performing the desired tasks. All of these methods have been adopted at one time or another by successful managers, and it may be necessary to switch from one method to another as situations change.

Power people must be prepared to maintain power. They must make few mistakes because a mistake will allow someone also on the lookout for power to take a step ahead. As a result they must take the usual rules of business—to set objectives within the limits of resources, and to chose the correct alternatives and then chose the line of least resistance, establish flexibility in both aims and objectives, and attempt to confuse the opposition with each step.

Once power has been obtained, it must be kept by constant vigilance, and this creates a problem for the manager. Time, off and on the job, is required to maintain power and to fend off those who are trying to wrest it from the present holder. But if too much time is invested in this procedure, the organization will suffer, and this leads to a decrease in power. A constant balancing act is essential.

Power can be gained in several ways. McCormack, one of America's most successful entrepreneurs, has said one of the best ways to obtain power is by doing favors. [7] Favors are of typically of three kinds: short-term favors which are usually ignored, lasting favors which are appreciated and contribute to the donees capability, and favors which make major differences in improved performance of the recipient.

Another obvious means of obtaining power is to secure a competitive edge on an opponent. The edge may be obtained by a variety of methods, but the most valuable lies in understanding the opponent better than he/she understands you. This involves: getting more and better facts, using intuition and imagination, knowing the situation and the players better than an opponent, using any crises to advantage, and waiting for a decison rather than forcing one.

The Japanese have excelled at these methods, while the American executive has made little effort to understand the power structure and behavioral patterns especially in Japan and thus has been able to make few inroads into the Japanese market. [8]

This boils down to one word—discipline. In addition, every business executive needs luck, but luck is often produced by power rather than by happenstance. It has been said with justification that luck is the reward of diligence.

The ability to negotiate offers one means of obtaining power. The powerful know what is wanted, when it is wanted it and for how long, where the decision is to be, and how much is to be sacrificed for it. The ability to make decisions may depend upon the ability of the executive to negotiate in less obvious ways:

1. Allowing the other side to go first in order to learn their position.
2. Avoiding showdowns.
3. Trading places in the mind's eye with the other side in order to understand their position.
4. Sweetening any deal with extraneous offers which do not detract from the main goal.
5. Assigning a definite time frame for decisions.
6. Being candid.
7. Using emotions to sway decisions.

Negotiation confers power automatically because it enables one to win. In addition, the executive who would wield power successfully must also be prepared to take advantage of bad timing on the part of an adversary, to take advantage of the best possible bargain that can be obtained, and to weigh the advantages of a decision on the far future as well as on the present. Negotiations are begun from a position of strength or weakness and the type of negotiation depends upon the ability of the executive to recognize the position of power. Failure to assess the situation accurately may lead to dramatic failure. The steps in the process can be easily followed in the financial and front pages of the daily paper.

One other attribute is essential. The wily executive seeking power must be unpredictable. The predictable person can be easily played out of position by a smart associate. Again, notice the reluctance with which one company reveals it is planning a takeover of another.

The search for power is the same regardless of whether an individual or a country is involved. Negotiations with the Soviet Union about the withdrawal of troops from Afghanistan are little different from the executive working with a union trying to obtain a pay raise. The same principles apply. There is little point here in discussing game theory, the basis of much of the discussion, but the reader should be aware there is a theoretical base for the power struggle.

A summary of the rules to obtain power would be to know the rules and how to use them, learn to use peers as allies rather than enemies, learn the system and how to manipulate it, and inspire trust in peers and overlords and loyalty in other workers. Power must be earned; it is seldom granted. And above all, power must be used for good (however defined) or bad (evil?) and only society can define which is which. The collusion between constituents and a congressman, such as that revealed in the recent information on the speaker of the House of Representatives, Jim Wright, where untold billions were secured for friends and associates, is not a crime in the halls of Congress but might well be so in other circumstances.

Unfortunately, power has become so great a factor in the business world that one can argue that it is used more for personal aggrandizement than for the good of society. The recent books on the Wall Street scandals have pointed out one fact—each manager attempts to gain power by stock manipulation for his personal gain. The stockholders were not a consideration in the ploys.

Education is one means of obtaining power. Knowledge is power and the days of the back room inventor are gone. Power is not so evident in education itself. True, the textbooks are determined by consensus vote, as witness the recent debate on the amount of evolution to be taught in schools. In college, power shifts more to the individual. Here, the individual who can obtain large research grants has power in the department and the university. Teaching may be neglected or relegated to graduate students, departmental duties may be handed to others, and the power of the dollar assures promotion and pay. This may be a disadvantage for training managers and scientists of tomorrow. In the laboratory a student may be relegated to a small area of a large problem and not have the opportunity to observe the development of a science. In business school, the same ideas apply. This can be contrasted with the Japanese manager who is trained in every aspect of the business. With the big growth of science and technology, we will never again see the Renaissance man who was knowledgeable in all things but we should encourage a broader outlook on the part of our young who may have to function in a global economy with technology not yet conceived. So from another viewpoint, power is education. Knowledge of the enemy, of friends, and of methodology provides the power base for decision making.

REFERENCES

1. R. G. H. Siu, *The Craft of Power*. New York: John Wiley and Sons, 1979.
2. P. Benchley, *Q Clearance*. New York: Random House, 1986.
3. J. M. Ivancevich, J. H. Donnelly, and J. L. Gibson, *Managing for Performance*. Dallas, Tex.: Business Publications, 1980.
4. D. Halberstam, *The Reckoning*. New York: Avon Press, 1987.
5. H. Smith, *The Power Game*. New York: Random House, 1988.
6. K. Boulding, *Conflict and Defense*. New York: Harper and Row, 1962.
7. M. H. McCormack, *What They Don't Teach You at Harvard Business School*. New York: Bantam Books, 1984.
8. S. Ikari, "The Japanese Work Ethic," *Sumitomo Corporation Bulletin*, Summer 1989, p. 21.
9. A. Toffler, *The Power Shift*. New York: Bantam Books, 1990.

11

Ethics and Excellence

The United States is gradually becoming an unethical country. Wall Street has suffered from major breaches of morality in the last few years, and such large companies as Chrysler have been censored for selling used cars as new vehicles. These examples may be reprehensible as isolated examples, but in the long run the ethics are determined by the ethos of a population. And we are seeing a deterioration in ethics from school to industry. Ethics are important. They prevent a rip-off of the consumer and taxpayer. They permit communication on an open basis between individuals and countries. They reduce the cost of doing business.

Ethical behavior is based on a number of precepts. Empirical behavior theory states ethics are evolved from the human experience and behavior and are agreed upon by general understanding. There is some basis for this statement. Cannibals may use human flesh as a sort of religious offering and to them it is ethical. The Ik, a primitive African tribe has difficulty surviving in the environment they live in and see nothing wrong about reducing the population by starving the very young or the very old. These facts lead to the conclusion that ethics derived by empiricism must be sane, rational, quantified, and measurable in the population adopting them.

However, ethics occupies a larger realm than mere fact. Rational ethical theory is the belief that people reason about what is good and bad and thus create ethics. The rational theory may take into account such matters as wishful thinking, propaganda and brainwashing, cultural inheritance, and peer group pressure. One subset among rational theorists believes that ethics are derived from the situation at hand, thus the Ik attitudes mentioned above.

Intuitive theory is belief that people possess a basic knowledge of what is right and wrong and would behave correctly in each situation if it were not for environment in an all-inclusive sense. This idea in one sense makes each person a law unto himself and such an attitude cannot exist for long in any state except anarchy. Still, most people use a blend of rational and intuitive theory with a smattering of empirical input to reach decisions on ethics. Finally, revelation theory says all ethics come from God.

In many cases we may find it difficult to separate the rule of law, ethics, and religion. They have become intertwined in the Judeo-Christian society so that they are intermixed and almost inseparable. The continuing discourse about the "right to life" is a case in point. This discussion on morals is founded in religion and supplemented by law. Many other examples could be cited.

It has been said with some justice, "Ethics is the small voice that tells us what other people should do." For this reason alone it is difficult indeed to set standards for ethical conduct. The standards of today are different from those of Victorian England and still further from those of Greece in the Golden Age. Attributes contributing to morals can be identified but it is hard to blend them into a code of ethics. Such attributes might include:

    1. Wisdom—without some sense of intelligence there can be no morals.
    2. Courage—ability to "stick to one's guns" is critical to maintain a moral code.
    3. Temperance—extremes almost never become part of moral code. The exception may be the religious attitude of the Muslim radicals.
    4. Justice—all moral codes are embedded in some concept of justice but the criteria of justice has varied from time to time.
    5. Conscience—the intuition of what is wrong or right developed by environmental contexts.

There has always been an argument about what is right or wrong about business ethics. The Jews were persecuted for usury in the Middle Ages both because of imagined avariciousness and for religious motives. A.Z. Carr has argued that business ethics are different from every-day morals and cannot be considered on the same ground.[1] He points out that one would never think of being honest about demands or restrictions in a labor negotiation before the bargaining started. George Bernard Shaw carried the moral idea to extremes. He argued that any profession is a conspiracy against the public. He has a point: specialists in medicine receive about 30 percent more income than the general practitioner and there is little evidence that they provide better care for the average disease. Becker and Fritsch tested the ethics of business people in several countries and found the range of what was considered to be good conduct varied considerably among countries.[2] This bears out the idea that ethics is in the eye of the beholder.

Ethics in business has been extended in recent years to the concept of community service. The industries of the Houston region provide millions of dollars of support to the arts. However, many individuals, including such wellknown economists as the Nobel prize winner Milton Friedman, have said that such activity is certain to destroy our free society and that business should exist for only one purpose, to make money. He is not alone. The Carthaginian Creed, stated more than 2,000 years ago, "Nothing is disgraceful if it results in a profit." This means that a dichotomy exists in the business world. Should business make money at all costs, or should business devote itself to the public good at almost all costs? We have mentioned that businesses are now changing their attitudes. The steel companies are in many areas of business other than steel, and steel has become an unimportant part of the portfolio. Automobile companies have diversified into many areas—all in the chase of the dollar. Does an industry have any responsibility other than to make money at all cost? It has been said with justification that the American auto industry has let the accountant run the company, and manufacturing and quality control have taken a back seat in the interest of profits. Probably both extreme views of the business as a philanthropic organization and as a quick profit structure are wrong, but a middle path may be hard to establish. What is the limit of corporate responsibility? Should a corporation provide day care centers to employee's children even when the cost decreases profits? Should a product of inferior quality be made if the public has no way to know it is inferior? To what extent should a corporation involve clients or the public in decisions? Many a dictatorship has been founded on the rule, "I know best what is good for them." Should the public be manipulated for its own "good"? And who decides good? The tobacco industry provides an excellent example of producing a dangerous product. President Ronald Reagan's administrative decisions supposedly taken for the public good by members of the White House staff turned out not to be in the public interest.

And finally, is the corporation more important than the individual? Here again, the Japanese quality circle concept has changed the approach of the corporation toward its workers. In 1979 the Ford motor company produced 4.5 million cars and made about $1.5 billion in profit with 500,000 workers. In 1986 the Ford company made 3.5 million cars with 380,000 workers and made the same profit. Was this ethical? In America the big changes are made in the auto industry by moguls who decide what the public wants and then provides it. In Japan more than 1,000 changes per year are made on cars directly as a result of ideas generated from the workers. These changes are each small but they add up to a greater quality. There is little wonder the Japanese have a loyalty to the company for which they work while in the United States the worker has no such loyalty. It has been said that when a worker in Detroit was asked why he worked four days a week his reply was, "Because I can't make a living working three days a week." And this situation is not unique. An announcement was recently made in Korea that workers would now work only 6 days a week instead of seven, indicating the trend to greater affluence. The Japanese are slowly shifting to a shorter work week but they have managed to maintain company loyalty. Is one attitude more ethical than another?

A survey by the *Institute of Electrical and Electronic Engineers' Spectrum* presenting three dilemmas to engineers and asking for opinions about ethics drew a widely varying response.[3] In one example, the ethics of marshaling only a few good units to be seen and tested by a potential buyer when the assembly line does not produce an acceptable quality of product was debated. An IBM manager suggested that the practice was not reprehensible if the deficiency could be corrected, while others suggested that honesty was the best policy. In another case production was yielding only 10 percent of maximum acceptable product, but some engineers still thought it was honest not to reveal this to a customer. In a third case a new device produced 50 percent duds in manufacture. In this case most of the engineers thought this fact should be reported, but some remarked that a scientist's opinion may be deferred by higher management in order to meet a deadline. These ideas have been borne out in the pharmaceutical industry where drugs with known serious side effects have continued to be produced in the name of profit.

Although we would agree the corporation as a whole should have some ethical values, it is the managers who set the tone for the ethical structure. Fulmer has posed several interesting problems indicating clearly the problems facing managers in making ethical decisions. [4]

1. Should a manager invest in a competing company?
2. Should a manager accept gifts for special favors?
3. Should a manager do business with an unethical firm?
4. Should a manager recruit an employee from a competitor?
5. Should a manager create artificial situations to keep employees on their toes?

These are only a few of many such problems that could be posed. The responses were different with the young as opposed to the older executive who appears to be more ethical in business dealings. When we consider the recent problems on Wall Street with young business executives and behind-the-counter dealing that has appeared, we can appreciate the difference.

The difference in the morals of the age is also affecting the professions that have had standards of conduct for thousands of years. Physicians and lawyers are being accused of a search for money rather than help for clients, for overpricing and rendering poor service. All of these can be documented in the case of the physician, in Chapter 12. Reports indicate rapidly increasing sloppy research work damaging the R and D efforts of universities and companies. This may not be outright cheating or unethical conduct, but it indicates an indifference in attitude pervading our culture.

With the rise of technology a new brand of ethicism is arising. The modern company with a technology background develops many products or procedures as trade secrets. The question of ethics arises when a manager forsakes one company for another and takes information with him. How much information is permissible? The definition of a trade secret is not set by a given law. Each state has its own definition.

Whereas copyrights and patents are regulated nationwide by the federal government, the trade secret has no legal definition. In general a trade secret is not available in published material. Once it has been revealed all proprietary interest is lost. In many companies, inventors, researchers, and others may be required to sign a contract agreeing not to reveal trade secrets, but the definitions are vague. In some states when an employee invents something on his own time and with his own equipment, it belongs to him, but if any of the employer's facilities are used, the invention may be in a very gray area. Nevertheless, there have been numerous court cases involving the employee who left a company with trade secrets and supposedly revealed them to a competitor. In several cases, a group of employees left to form a company in direct competition to the parent. This creates a problem of what is permissible to take and what must be left behind. Lawyers have said the best ethical and legal position for an employee is to take nothing on departure. This may be difficult when the ideas are present and it is often hard to avoid using them in another context. Yet Ross Perot left Electronic Data Systems (EDS) to form a company to study the post office and took several key executives with him. As he had formed EDS in the first place, had employed the executives and set the goals and objectives for the company, was his move ethical? EDS believes it was not and has sued to prevent the moves employed by Perot.

Failure to be ethical may result in lawsuits, and it may go further. Several companies have been accused of destroying a company set up by former employees even when no violation of trade secrets was known to be involved.

The moral code may be hard for the employee to digest, but it is also difficult for most companies. There is little wonder. It has been difficult even for the churches to remain blameless when they should set the moral standard. The furor about the PTL Club and the financial ethics of Jim and Tammy Bakker have recently been in the news. The actions of the IRS to require tax payments from churches that own and operate large businesses is another indication all is not well in the religious sector.

Nevertheless, every business should have a code, and it should be clearly visible. Establishment of a code must be a company-wide activity. One person cannot set the code for the organization and expect all employees to abide by it. Participation brings the needed support. The code must be clearly published and totally enforced. A code permitting one thing in one situation and something else in another almost identical situation is an indication to the employee that the strings are loose and considerable play will be allowed. And the code must be modifiable as circumstances demand.

Such a code will provide advantages for the customer who understands that the product generates confidence for the industry that must deal with the company or enforce industry-wide codes, and for the executive because the people with whom he/she deals will respect judgment and honesty.

There is always the question of what the executive should do in the face of unethical practices. R.P. Nielsen has discussed the options.[5] He mentions a few steps to take:

1. Don't think about it.
2. Go along with the rest.
3. Object.
4. Leave.
5. Secretly or publicly blow the whistle.
6. Threaten to reveal information.
7. Sabotage the plan.
8. Build a consensus against the plan in the organization.

Let us now turn from generalizations about ethics to specific examples. The ethics of the individual executive and of the organization as a whole have come into question. Lee Iacocca refused to travel in anything but an expensive private jet while at Chrysler, although the jet was paid for by the funds of the American taxpayer while the government was bailing Chrysler out of bankruptcy. Senate hearings revealed that LTV went into Chapter 11 bankruptcy to avoid paying pension funds for the workers in its plants and thus allowed the taxpayer to pay for LTV pensions. The leveraged buyouts of large firms so prevalent on Wall Street may make huge sums for the buyers or sellers, but they are often paid for with junk bonds with little value in the future and thus disadvantage the stockholder. The failure of hundreds of savings and loan associations in the Southwest and elsewhere has been said to result from greed, downright dishonesty, and chicanery with the lender's funds in more than 50 percent of the cases. And the government is not exempt. An agency in Texas handing out payments at a below poverty level for the poor has been accused of spending thousands of dollars for office furniture for the director. The cost overruns for $100 screwdrivers and $1,000 toilet seats by the Pentagon have become a national scandal. Thousands of other examples could be cited. None of these actions could be considered very ethical. Such cases may not be very different from other companies who in the name of economy have trimmed back benefits the worker may be forced to accept. The attempts of Continental Airlines to break unions to reduce personnel costs and documented cases of insurance companies raising malpractice fees by 300 percent when there were no increases in cases or awards are other examples of the malaise of the country.

Walter Reuther, admittedly a biased observer, once said the history of free enterprise in the auto industry was to raise prices in response to competition. This is certainly borne out in an earlier statement in this book taken from Halberstam suggesting Ford laid off 130,000 workers while increasing profits of the corporation. Such practices border on the unethical, depending on how workers were handled.[6]

It behooves American industry to examine its motives and its challenges. The public is becoming more and more aware of the ethical problems and is beginning to demand change. The recent prosecution of many Wall Street traders is a case in point. The public no longer believes claims about quality in American industry, and the auto industry in fact has switched from advertising quality to advertising low interest rates on automobile loans. The much-advertised Sterling car as the epitome of perfection has many flaws according to *Consumer Reports*. Each executive must make choices and in the same situation many different solutions may be tried. When Richard Nixon attempted to fire the prosecutor in the Watergate case, Elliot Richardson resigned rather than execute the order but others were found to execute it.

Aircraft companies have been accused of major lapses in ethics. Despite massive overruns on costs, the Government Accounting Office (GAO) has charged Rockwell International with improprieties in the construction of the B-1 bomber including fuel leaks because of poor construction, failure to build electronics to specifications, and other problems that can be corrected only by a major redesign of the aircraft. Hedrick Smith in his erudite book on Washington politics, *The Power Game,* says that Rockwell has established parts of its contracting to build the B-1 bomber in 400 of 435 congressional districts with the aim of influencing defense legislation. Some 13,000 defense employees and military officers with the contracting division of the Department of Defense have gone to work for the industry they were supervising, and often in the same area where they were overseeing industry operations. Is this ethical? Is this the pork barrel in the sky? It has been documented that the Department of Defense with collusion of aircraft manufacturers has let contracts and testified to Congress on low costs of military equipment knowing the costs would be higher and the overruns could be adjusted by change orders. There is a question of ethics within the Department of Defense. We now have more generals on duty in the Pentagon than we had at the height of World War II despite diminishing threats everywhere except in the Middle East, and about one-sixth of the World War II military force on duty. Is this ethical? In the same light, one may well wonder if the troubles of NASA with lost craft, failures of flights, and poor performances of the Hubble telescope in the nineties were not a part of the same syndrome.

The government and industry have not been excoriated alone for decline of ethics. The educational system follows a close second. Cheating is rampant at all levels in the school system, and the teachers' unions maintain poor and incompetent teachers at a sacrifice to the education of the young. The subject matter is subjected to an attempted revision on the part of strict religionists and the material taught is not of high caliber.

Medical ethics is also undergoing scrutiny. The vast majority of physicians are ethical in the practice of medicine, but they indulge in methods unethical at the extremes. Is it ethical to place a person in an intensive care unit (ICU) for days at costs now approaching $1,000 per day when there is no hope of recovery or when less intensive care would suffice? Is it ethical to prolong or save the life of an infant when its medical and surgical problems will place a burden on the family and the taxpayers for years into the future with little hope of survival into adulthood? Recent data suggests that children are now growing up with twice the number of serious defects of several years ago as a result of medical intervention. And such children place a burden on the medical system, the educational system, and the social system. For the same degree of health as measured by mortality statistics, the surgeons in the United States perform three times as many hysterectomies, twice as many prostatectomies, and many more surgical operations in general than surgeons in any other developed country. Should this raise ethical questions? The Office of Technology Assessment of the Congress has reported that kidney dialysis centers operated for a profit dialyze many more patients (the elderly, the comatose, and others) than actually need the treatment, and the large centers equipped with the modern scanning devices—Magnetic Nuclear Resonance, Computerized Axial Tomography, and others, test many patients where the technology is ineffective.

The present health care system is oriented toward treatment of disease after it occurs rather than prevention of disease for a better quality of care. We attempt to correct heart disease by heart transplants and cardiac bypass surgery rather than correcting the diet and stopping the sale of tobacco, which would be cheaper and more effective. And this process raises another ethical question. Is it proper to allow some patients who can raise $100,000 to have a heart transplant while bypassing the rest of the population who may need the treatment but cannot afford it?

There is now an awakening on the part of industry and the patient to some of the abuses in the medical system. Industry is creating health mintenance organizations (HMO's) to provide selective, cheaper care to workers. Second opinions on the use of surgery and other procedures is becoming routine as a result of pressure on the insurance companies. Patients are raising questions about "the right to die" or to "pull the plug" on incurable patients rather than to maintain them on life support systems. Most of the discussion has centered around medical ethics as a result of commission of actions. There are also sins of omission. Most doctors do not practice preventive medicine because it is not to their advantage to do so. Most are unaware of public health measures such as protection from chemicals, atmospheric conditions and other adverse conditions, or the general prevention of disease. Over and above the ethical questions suggested above, there are questions of actual misconduct. Many physicians have been sued by the government for Medicaid fraud in false billing, overtreating, and overprescribing of drugs.

Industry as a whole has many problems. A recent survey by Sandrof found that 70 percent of employees were aware of nepotism in their employers, 67 percent were aware of unfair credit taking, 62 percent were aware of being lied to about the company activity, and 52 percent knew of stealing in the company.[7] When the survey examined the professional locations of the reporters, it was found that 66 percent of complaints occurred in the government, 51 percent in the sales force, 40 percent in law firms, and 38 percent in the media. This data suggests that the ethics of business are not very good.

We are slowly destroying our environment, and that also is an ethical problem. Should automobile manufacturers be allowed to continue to pollute the atmosphere with carbon monoxide and to produce hundreds of thousands of tons of nitrous oxides, destroying the protective elements of the atmosphere and threatning the world with a changed climate, when better engines are possible? Should factories be allowed to dump acid into rivers and lakes to create destruction and pollute the atmosphere with acid rain? Should the farmer be allowed to use excessive amounts of fertilizer and water, depleting the resources of the country out of proportion to the good they create?

The list goes on and on. We must face these problems with money, with legislation, and with a new set of ethical values that will not permit the excesses of the past. Any attempt to change the situation has been futile. Industry as a whole unethical mass has successfully fought many of the proposals that would benefit society and through collusion has obtained the help of Congress. A few items will illustrate the problem.

Tobacco is still in production and subsidized by the Department of Agriculture although the medical problems have been amply demonstrated. Factories around the Great Lakes are still polluting the atmosphere despite a lawsuit from Canada. Although other developed countries have suggested environmental controls the United States has refused to date to consider them, citing a disbelief in the data despite substantiation delivered by the National Academy of Sciences. Automobile manufacturers have fought every attempt to reduce emissions from engines, usually successfully. Physicians have fought HMOs, second opinions on surgery, and other restrictive laws with some success. Farmers have resisted any attempt to reduce water supply for unneeded crops and have fought successfully in Congress for additional dams, canals, and water sources.

In summary, we suggest that the ethics of our society are deteriorating in government, education, and business. We have not established norms for good behavior and forced adherence to them. One of the major reasons is that norms must be established by law through Congress, and Congress is under suspicion of defending pork barrel politics, taking gifts from lobbyists, indulging in conflict of interest activity in many instances, and worrying about reelection to the detriment of the political process of law making.

REFERENCES

1.   A. Z. Carr, "Is Business Bluffing Ethical?" *Harvard Business Review,* January 1968, p. 143.

2.   H. Becker and D. J. Fritzsche, "Business Ethics," *J. of Business Ethics* 6:289 (1987).

3.   D. Christiansen, "Ethical Dilemmas Revisited," *IEEE Spectrum* 26 (4):21 (April 1989).

4.   R. M. Fulmer, *The New Management.* 4th ed. New York: Macmillan, 1987.

5.   R. P. Nielsen, "What Can Managers Do about Unethical Management?" *J. of Business Ethics* 6:309 (1987).

6.   D. Halberstam, *The Reckoning*. New York: Avon Press, 1987.

7.   R. Sandroff, "How Ethical Is American Business?" *Working Woman,* September 1990, p. 113.

12

Health Care—
A Problem Enterprise

The health care system is a remarkable conglomeration of factors of education, technology, and finance. Many of its problems are the result of the educational system and the kind of training which the physician receives. The technology increases exponentially in both cost and complexity, and there is considerable question as to whether it results in better or poorer care. Management is divided between physicians and business people and the dichotomy results in poor management. Any attempt to change the system for the better must be firmly rooted in the reeducation of the management, the physician, and the consumer.

The industry as a whole has many of the same problems of poor management, lack of innovative management, and failure to take advantage of opportunity that beset the rest of the industrial effort of the United States. The health care industry is a study of contradiction. On one hand it has a high degree of excellence in the actual delivery of medical care while on the other it suffers from poor quality and lack of excellence when measured in terms of outcomes for expenditures, failure to provide care to everyone, and mistaken goals. Moreover, the health care industry has more problems than most industries in that it suffers under a dual management structure (the financial and structural management and the medical management) which is often in conflict, a greater degree of supervision by the government, and a greater accountability to the public. All these problems tend to create an inefficient and poorly managed system.

These factors affect the community directly. The hospital and the physician always charge on a cost-plus basis, and, as the cost of health care rises, so does the cost to maintain health plans for employees. When the cost of health care plans is rising at twice the rate of the cost of living, it behooves the prudent manager to examine the reason for such costs and what can be done about them. A discussion of health care must take at least two tacks. An improvement in efficiency that may benefit the physician and the hospital may provide negative benefit to the consumer using the system. If the hospital increases its cash flow, which might be considered a measure of improved efficiency, it must come from the pockets of the consumer. On the other hand, decreased costs to the consumer in terms of tax reduction or lower insurance premiums for payment of health care may result in poor care, so that effort must be taken to maintain quality.

Only three elements must be considered in depth in examining the health care system—the hospital, the physician, and the patient. The three are intermixed in a matrix of operations which must also be considered. We will consider each of the three in turn.

THE HOSPITAL

The rapidly increasing costs of hospital care have been a matter of concern. The costs continue to rise at twice the cost of living index or the GNP.[1] Hospital administrators refer to efficiency of their operations in terms of better cleaning procedures or better collection of debts rather than "more bang for the buck" in total overall efficiency. It is possible to improve productivity in the hospital by better scheduling, improvement in food services, and personnel management. But these are relatively trivial when compared to the other costs.

The major factor which would lower costs immediately would be the elimination of excess beds. Overbedding is serious and a major cause of low productivity. Present estimates are that the beds are about 65 percent occupied in the total system, and hospital chains are still building additional beds. Methodist Hospital in Houston is adding an addition of hundreds of beds while the average occupancy of hospital beds in Houston is about 55 percent. The productivity loss is apparent. Unoccupied beds cost about 65 percent of the cost of an occupied bed and return no revenue. Hospital administrators make the point that such beds are available in case of emergency, but this is a specious argument and the inhouse patients pay for the empty beds with increased daily costs. The community has not been educated to the reasons for costs in health care and the ways to reduce the costs. One is to reduce numbers of beds.

The hospital could also control the operations of its physician staff with a tighter hand.[2]   A review of the physician's use of surgery, a review of the pathology reports to see how much unnecessary surgery is performed, and a closer review of the laboratory usage would all reduce costs.

Each of these services returns a hefty income to the hospital, and any restriction is opposed by the hospital administrators. A restriction on the overuse of drugs or the laboratory also would result in lost income and is opposed for similar reasons. Strangely enough, there appears to be little correlation between the amount of technology and fancy operative procedures in the hospital and the quality of care. The large hospital makes a point of the additional service that can be provided, but investigators have found that there is an optimum size for a hospital and when it reaches above about 600 beds inefficiencies begin to creep in which interfere with the quality of care. As an example, it costs a 700-bed hospital $7,100 per year to keep an empty bed open, while the same bed costs in a 200-bed hospital are less than $5,000.

The modern technology on which the hospital banks to attract staff and furnish income has not greatly improved treatment. It is possible that the last 1 percent of diagnoses are improved at a 100 percent increase in costs, but this is an inefficient use of resources. As an example, the National Cancer Institute reported in 1985 that with the exception of children's cancer, there had been no significant improvement in cancer cures for at least ten years as measured by survival rates. Cancer of the testes, skin, bladder, and prostate have improved marginally while lung, blood, colon, and cervical cancers have decreased rates of survival. Yet billions of dollars continue to be spent on cancer treatment with the most expensive technology. There is a strong reminder of the Detroit industries continuing to build big cars after the mind of the public changed.

The hospital faces insatiable demands from the physician for new technology. Physicians have been educated in medical school to use the latest technology and to regard other means of treatment as outmoded. We have barely discovered that the computerized axial tomography (CAT) scanners do not do all that they should in diagnosis before the medical community is demanding magnetic nuclear resonance (MNR) and positron emission tomography (PET) scanners. A reduction in the cost of high technology would materially improve the productivity.

The hospital is inefficient in other ways. The creation of intensive care units (ICUs) draws resources from other areas. Some teaching hospitals with as many as ten ICUs may spend 25 percent of total resources on less than 5 percent of the patients. An examination of need for an ICU and a closer scrutiny of the type of patient and their real need might well reduce costs substantially.[3],[4] The hospital may generate as much as 20 percent of income from the 2 percent of patients placed in the units at a cost of more than $1,000 a day. The problem is that the best indications are that about 85 percent of the patients are not improved by the experience and Bloom has said that many come out of the unit sicker than when they entered it.[5] Kolata in a series of articles in *Science* has pointed out the high cost and low return in health improvement for kidney dialysis centers, heart transplant centers, and the like.[6]

The hospital is also a dangerous place to be ill. Patients suffer from iatrogenic diseases of mistaken treatment, drug reactions, electrical shocks, falls, and other trauma in the hospital. Of all malpractice judgments 87 percent are against hospitals for negligence in patient care. Unfortunately, patients are not trained to recognize poor treatment. Great trust is placed in the physicians and their medical decisions.

We have mentioned the laboratory. As Cerullo has pointed out, an analysis of information flow and services provided by the laboratory might reduce costs to the patient.[7] The hospital encourages laboratory use because it is the single most lucrative element with the possible exception of radiology. Again, the patient is not educated to request generic drugs or to question drug use by the physician.

There is considerable question as to whether the method of handling the health care of the aged through hospitalization is the method of choice, although it is certainly the method most widely used.[4] We may question the rise of more than 35 percent in cost of hospitalization for the aged when the rise in admissions for the general population is less than 10 percent in the same period and this is considered to be too high. New forms of centers for the aged are now coming to the fore to remedy this situation.

THE PHYSICIAN

The physician clearly bears a considerable responsibility for cost containment and improvement in productivity. The possibilities for improvement have many ramifications. For example, Eisenberg has pointed out that the simple review of diagnostic procedures by colleagues or superiors will markedly reduce costs.[2] Others have called attention to the overuse of surgery as an elective procedure in the United States as compared to Europe and even Canada and have suggested a tightened review of surgical cases.

Physicians have consistently refused to use cost-saving measures in practice. The cost-saving use of nurse practitioners, physicians' assistant, and the like have spread slowly and then only in those areas of the profession such as pediatrics where there is a clear profit to the physician. There is clear evidence that the costs of care can be reduced with such assistance, but under the present conditions of oversupply of physicians, there is unlikely to be any attempt to use a cheaper pair of hands to deliver health care.

The value of measuring diagnostic efficiency, which measures the ability to make a diagnosis, and therapeutic efficiency, which measures the effectiveness with which treatment has been provided, has never been considered. By the same measure, physicians have also not considered the value of not doing a test or procedure. Robin found that screening for cancer of the pancreas requires a dangerous test and more patients may die as a result of the test than would die of the cancer, yet the tests continue.[8]

Laboratory tests may create major problems. It is reliably estimated that thousands of physicians have laboratories in their offices where tests are performed routinely. Some of these inhouse laboratories perform as many as 10,000 tests annually and when it is considered that the average test costs about $20, the return to the physician is obvious. In many of these laboratories nurses run the tests with no controls and few checks on accuracy. Senator Edward Kennedy, a few years ago, held hearings on the inhouse laboratory and found that more than 70 percent of the tests were inaccurate, many dangerously so; that values ranged widely between laboratories and that nurses were often not well trained to perform the test.[9] Nowadays much of the laboratory equipment is highly automated with sophisticated electronics so that unseen errors may creep into analysis. In addition, commercial kits make easy tests readily available and the efficacy of some of the kits is in question. The FDA has withdrawn kits from the market because of inaccurate results. However, physicians claim that the inhouse laboratory permits rapid assessment of patients and prevents return visits. Congress is sufficiently concerned to consider an Omnibus Health Bill which will regulate the use of inhouse laboratories by the physician.

These are only examples of poor quality control, but well illustrate the pervasive nature of the problem. It is no different from quality control of parts manufacture in industry although the consequences may be more dangerous.

In better control but equally egregious is the practice of the physician owning laboratories and pharmacies. The quality control may be better because trained professionals are employed to operate the business but there is the tendency to order more tests or more drugs to increase income. Thousands of doctors own stock in or operate hospitals, clinics, labs, and other medical businesses. Such a practice is encouraged in industry because the employee or public has a stake in the business and will work to make it succeed, while in health care such a practice may run up the costs without improving the outcomes.

In addition, the physician is a law unto himself and this creates different standards of care in different areas of the country. The clearly demonstrated differences in length of hospital stays and the differences in rate of surgical procedures in the various sections is a case in point. When one county in a state averages three times as many hysterectomies as another, when one section of the country keeps patients in the hospitals 40 percent longer than another section, there is good reason to raise questions about productivity. When these aberrations are correlated with oversupply of beds and physicians as they usually are, the problem becomes more acute.[1]

The medical system has relied on technology since the invention of the stethoscope. The trend continues even when there is no clear benefit to be derived from it. It has been found, for example, that there is no significant advantage in the use of fetal monitoring in normal deliveries which comprise a major portion of all deliveries. Yet fetal monitoring is used in a high percentage of such cases. The mortality rate of infants is the same regardless of the use of monitoring. The evidence is clear that in many cases inhalation therapy, especially intermittent positive pressure breathing (IPPB) may do more harm than good to patients, yet some 30 percent of all patients admitted to the hospital are subjected to it.

These two examples of many suggest that productivity can be increased in the health care system. Several authors have attempted to deal with the problem and suggested means of control. Eisenberg has suggested that the physician be personally billed for all excess services ordered for a patient.[2] It has also been suggested that many of the services rendered on an inpatient basis could be provided equally well on an outpatient service without sacrificing quality of patient care. The federal government with a heavy stake in the costs of health care has created the professional review organizations (PRO) and utilization review (UR) procedures in an attempt to control costs. Both have been opposed by the physicians and the hospitals.

A major source of low productivity and therefore higher costs resides in the physician. The overuse of hospital beds for convenience, the overuse of technology, and the high charge all decrease productivity. In addition, the overproduction of physicians has resulted in increased costs. It has been estimated that the average physician costs the economy about $400,000 per year in health care costs. It has been suggested that a reduction in hospital beds should occur until a queue forms, placing the physician in the position of making hard decisions about admissions, which could increase productivity.

THE PATIENT

Lest we blame the health care system alone for the low productivity, we must recall that much of the cause of low productivity is the patient. As third party payment increases and as the employer bears more and more of the total costs of health care, the patient sees less and less of the total costs and therefore has no compunction about demanding more care. It is often the patient who demands the presence of a specialist when a nurse practitioner (NP) would be equally satisfactory, it is the patient who demands the CAT scan or the elaborate tests, and it is the pregnant mother who wants fetal monitoring. For this reason many employers are now turning to coinsurance as a means of disincentive to the use of the health care system.

The patient also increases the costs of the system in cooperation with the lawyer. Malpractice insurance is high and likely to go higher, and each suit increases the costs to the general public. It also increases the risks to the patient because the physician is likely to order more tests at greater risk for protection.

TECHNOLOGY IN HEALTH CARE

Technology has always been a part of medical care. Ancient Greek physicians used some sort of chemical test for urine, doctors in the eighteenth century began to use auscultation, and in the nineteenth century the X-ray, the electrocardiograph (ECG), and chemical analysis began to appear in hospitals. Within the last few years we have seen a burst of technology as new methods of analysis have been developed. Microelectronics has lead to the CAT scanner, the PET, MNR, the Autoanalyzer, and other complex and expensive tools.

It has been estimated that one CAT scanner is sufficient for a population of more than one million people, but in a large city every hospital worthy of the name will have at a least one machine and some will have many. In the Texas Medical Center there are four or five NMR machines in a two-block square area and others are being purchased for the reasons discussed above despite there being no clear demonstration of need.

In making goods, improvement in machines can produce a product faster or better than before, and the role of technology is obvious, but in health care, the application is not so apparent. In fact, it has only increased the cost to the patient, while reducing the time and energy that the physician spends on patient problems. The increase in technology has increased the number of persons required per patient to deliver health care in order to maintain the equipment and provide operating expertise the physician does not have. The loss in productivity is clear: the number of workers required to support a patient in the hospital has increased from one and one-third workers to almost four within twenty years. The use of technology in health care where it might actually improve productivity through research in operations, planning, and management, has not been well exploited. In fact, it has been pointed out that the major fault of the system in failing to increase productivity is due to faulty management with the resultant inappropriate strategies, poor quality control, poor resource management, and bad estimation of time scales. All of these are present in the health care system.

Financial management has also been poor in health care. Many people believe that the long-term aims of health care have been lost by both the hospital and the physician in their search for the dollar. The establishment of marketing departments in hospitals and for doctors to sell health care is a case in point. The proper attitude would be to sell a system of preventive health care or to decrease the available resources. Output of the system is measured in terms of hospital income and census rather than cure rate. This may not appear at first glance to be a problem of financial management, but the poor management is demonstrated by the rapid rise in costs per unit output as measured by patient turnover or patient wellness.

The health care system is a very large part of the economy of this country. The system with millions of employees and with a budget approaching $500 billion obviously affects the total economy. And the health care system is a poor producer. Health care costs increase about twice as fast as the cost of living in general, a good indication of poor productivity.

A problem in the health care system is the definition of performance. From the standpoint of the system per se, productivity might be measured by number of patients, number of beds built, number of tests run, and other work measures. But these are poor measures indeed when contrasted to the productivity of the system as measured by the outcome of patient care, the number of patients returned to good health, and the cost per patient for treatment. Dunnette has pointed-ed out that the definition of productivity depends to a large extent upon what is being measured and the results to be obtained.[10] By these measures the system is doing very well indeed. The number of employees increases steadily, the number of beds is increasing, the number of patients is increasing, and the cost per patient is increasing. From the standpoint of the patient the system is very poor. Fewer people are cured for each dollar invested, demands for increased costs grow year by year, and the cumbersome system contributes less and less to a sense of well-being of its use.

However, this cannot be compared directly to other industries. The auto manufacturer measures success in the number of cars and the steel maker measures the tons of steel produced, but neither measure can be used in the health care industry where it is almost impossible to comment on the costs, the efficiency, the quality, or the cost benefit of the product.

The health care system is one of the largest industries in the world. It employs millions of people and invests billions of dollars per year in growth and maintenance. The system is designed to provide service in the form of about 1 billion office calls to 300,000 practicing physicians each year and to provide for 300 million hospital days and 100 million patient days in nursing homes. In 1990 the current rate of inflation was about 5 percent per year but the increase in hospital costs is estimated to be about 9 percent. The total costs now approach $400 billion, of which the government in one form or another will pay about 40 percent. In 1983 we spent $342 billion on health care or about $1,400 per person. This figure will reach about $500 billion or $2,200 per person by 1991. The largest portion of the total cost is invested in hospital care. The physician accounts for about 25 percent of the costs, the nursing home for about 15 percent, and the hospital for 40 percent. The growth in physician charges increased almost twice as fast as hospital charges.[8] Medicare paid an average of $34,000 per physician in 1983 and some surgeons made as much as $75,000 per year from this source. More than 20 percent of all costs were expended for patients older than sixty-five years of age who received twice as much care as other groups in the population. Surgeries also increased twice as fast as the population. These figures change regularly. The present figures are taken from *Advance Data*, published at monthly intervals by the National Center for Health Statistics, Research Triangle, North Carolina.

In summary, when life span and contributions to society of the elderly are considered, the productivity of the system is poor. Great Britain has restricted medical care to the elderly on these grounds.

Goldfarb has pointed out that it is to the hospitals' advantage to optimize admissions, patient mix, and quality within constraints of technology and excess capacity.[11] These studies have been substantiated by many others who found that the major problem of productivity has been to correct the overcapacity with its resulting high costs. The hospital is operating on a cost-plus system. Charges are adjusted to meet expenses plus overhead plus profit. Voluntary hospitals complain about the losses from prospective payments but they fail to explain that those losses occur only after wings have been built, expensive equipment purchased, and overhead expanded.

The reason is that the hospital does not operate on a cost system but on a charge basis, and the charges may bear no relationship to the costs. In some departments such as the laboratory and radiology the charges are many times the costs, and a large profit is made. In housekeeping the costs may exceed the charges. Prospective reimbursement will produce some shifting of charges in order for the hospital to continue its production of net income.

Lest we reach the conclusion that the health care system is unique and does not relate to other businesses, we can summarize its problems in terms of management:

1. The personnel are not well dispersed and too many employees are doing the same job.

2. The management is not organized and is dispersed, so that the goals are not the same throughout the management structure.

3. Aims of the organization have turned from primary aims (health care) to profits.

4. Management is far removed from actual delivery of the service.

5. Quality suffers as a result of overemphasis on rate of production.

How many of these faults apply to industry in general as well as to the health care system?

SOME SOLUTIONS

Obviously, employers are seeking changes in the health care system to reduce the cost which in turn would result in greater productivity. We have mentioned that many employees now regard health care as a right, and unions negotiate for it as much as they do for salary. But the increases in cost are rapidly pricing the manager out of the market. In Houston estimates were for an 18 percent increase in medical insurance costs between 1987 and 1988 (*Houston Post*, February 5, 1989), and an average across the country of about 15 percent when the GNP is expected to rise about 1 percent and the total cost of living about 6 percent. One wonders what the cost of living (COL) would be if the health care cost increases were held to the general national COL rate. As a result of unreasonable cost increases in health care, new methods of providing health care have been developed and further experimentation is under way.

The obvious method is for industry to increase the deductible, which accomplishes two purposes: it reduces the direct cost and also reduces the overall cost for care because employees who have a healthy deductible tend to use less health care service. A second method is to go "bare" and attempt to hire professional staff to provide care at a cheaper cost within the company. A third method is to establish a professional provider organization (PPO) and contract for services with a group of physicians who work for set fees. Still another method is to establish a health maintenance organization (HMO) as Kaiser did many years ago. HMOs have been more or less successful. In general, an HMO must agree to a set of conditions for providing health care. Typically these specify that total health care will be provided by the organization at a fixed cost in specified locations. Usually total health care is provided and exclusions may be small. Emphasis is on prevention because in this way the organization can save money on treatment. Physicians are usually hired at a salary to provide services which are billed to the company or the employee through a salary deductible plan. State medical associations have objected strenuously to such a practice as they deem it to be the corporate practice of medicine, and thus against ethical standards, and it is forbidden by law in many states.

The PPO is not an HMO. The PPO is a group of physicians who provide health care but each is paid for his services (although the user may pay a fixed rate). Typically the PPO uses a local hospital with which it contracts to deliver beds as needed. There is less effort to encourage prevention because each physician still makes a living out of fees charged to the organization. The overall costs to the consumer may be less because a set of fees is agreed upon at the outset and this typically reduces costs.

The first HMO was set up by the Kaiser Company during World War II and provided total health care to Kaiser workers. The Kaiser Plan owned its own hospitals, hired physicians at a salary, and provided good health care at a reasonable cost. Some physicians object to this type of plan, deeming it the corporate practice of medicine, and complaining that it removes the physician from serving as an entrepreneur. The claim is made that the plans skimp on health care to save money, but the evidence is against that thesis. Consumers have the right to change plans at regular intervals, and if they are not satisfied, they may drop out of the system. Most evidence suggests that the number of patients actually increases over time, indicating satisfaction and that few drop out for cause.

The HMO has high start-up costs which may preclude its use in some organizations. The original cost may be several million dollars to build and equip hospitals or clinics, pay staff, and maintain empty beds before the patient load increases. The typical breakeven point occurs several years after establishment and requires an enrollment of about 25,000 or more in order to provide the range of services needed by an average community.

The HMO may also have trouble in breaking even depending upon the community. An HMO in industry typically has an enrollment of young, healthy adults (the workers), but one established by an entire community, for example, may have elderly, handicapped, and very ill individuals who run up the cost of care.

In the early years of HMO formation, the United States government paid for start-up costs and establishment in order to get the idea into widespread use. The HMO funded by government funds was required to be nondiscriminatory and this resulted in the failure of many systems as those clients who were otherwise uninsurable rushed to enter.

Joseph Califano, former Secretary of the Department of Health and Human Services, established an HMO at Chrysler in an attempt to reduce the high cost of medical services. He also wanted to pay for patient care while users were well and reduce payments while they were sick on the old Chinese principle that the physician's aim should be to keep the patient well. Although the proposal has merit, it has yet to be adopted.

Because of these problems, companies have been experimenting with health plans. Many companies offer a variety of plans ranging from PPO to fee-for-service, but some are aggressively trying to enroll patients (employees) in cost saving plans. The Bell System has a "Custom Care" plan which has many of the attributes of a PPO and is one of the most aggressive cost-reduction plans in the country, trying to make the employee health conscious and aware of the costs through intensive education. About 80 percent of Bell employees are signed up for the plan.

Texas Eastern has initiated educational programs on mental health, smoking, alcohol, drugs, and weight control, along with a nutrition program to reduce use of the health care plan. Some companies have policies of not hiring workers who drink, smoke, use drugs, or are more than 10 percent overweight.

Other companies have established smoke free workplaces in an attempt to reduce smoking and the disease associated with it. Most companies have now initiated dual review of major surgery, close monitoring of bills, and other cost containment. A more efficient cost-containment procedure, now being adopted by many industries with a large stake in the costs, has been to demand that hospitals be more efficient, that doctors monitor patients more closely for actual need for care, and that patients pay more deductibles. Industry is complaining that it is picking up the cost for vastly underutilized facilities. In addition, there is concern that some 20 percent of all claims by physicians and hospitals may be exaggerated or actually fabricated and represent a major overpayment of health care costs.

One of the problems is that the employees have had the best in a time of affluence, but as costs continue to rise, they must pay more or receive less service. How this will affect health care in the future and the cost of such care has not yet been decided.

REFERENCES

1. J. H. U. Brown, *The High Cost of Healing*. New York: Human Sciences Press, 1985.

2. J. M. Eisenberg and A. J. Rosoff, "Physician Responsibility for the Cost of Unnecessary Medical Services," *New England J. of Medicine* 299:76 (1978).

3. M. Pauly, "What Is Unnecessary Surgery?" *Millbank Memorial Fund Quarterly* 57:95 (1979).

4. L. B. Russell, *An Aging Population and the Use of Medical Care*. Washington, D.C.: Brookings Institution, 1981.

5. B. S. Bloom and O. L. Peterson, "End Results, Cost, and Productivity of Coronary-Care Units," *New England J. of Medicine* 288:72 (1973).

6. G. B. Kolata, "Withholding Medical Treatment," *Science* 205:882 (1979).

7.   M. J. Cerullo, "Smoothing Management Information Flow with Systems Analysis," *Hospital Financial Management* 33 (8):12 (August 1979).

8.   E. D. Robin, *Matters of Life and Death.* New York: W. H. Freeman, 1984.

9.   E. H. Kennedy, *Regulation of Clinical Laboratories: Hearings on S-1737.* Washington, D.C.: U.S. Government Printing Office, 1975.

10.   M. D. Dunnette and E. A. Fleishman, eds., *Human Performance and Productivity.* Hillsdale, N.J.: Lawrence Erlbaum Associates, 1982.

11.   National Center for Health Statistics, *Advance Data.* Washington, D.C.: U.S. Government Printing Office (published monthly).

12.   M. Goldfarb, M. Hornbook, and J. Rafferty, "Behavior of the Multiproduct Firm," *Medical Care* 18:185 (1980).

13

The Executive and the Work Group

The previous chapters dealt with the problems of educating the work force. Commentary on the faults without some indication of methods of changing the system would be useless. For example, there are indications that American business is changing, although very slowly. The rewards of the executive are being altered.[1] A very large portion of all executives are still paid by salary, but the use of stock options and rewards based on company profits are now more common. Still, less than 50 percent of all firms use any nontraditional reward.

However, with changing times, the situation must change. It has been pointed out that in times of stagnant productivity and fierce international competition, the reward system must change to reward for services rendered as measured by some objective standard.[2] The report of a White House conference goes on to say that the attitudes of employees are changing. Many are now asking for a hand in decision making and assurance of job security in preference to the usual wage increases. All suggest that fundamental changes must occur in organizations at all levels, and the next major thrust into the executive ranks will be pay for performance.

Along with the question of job security must come the uneasiness of knowing that reduction of staff is inevitable in the search for productivity and efficiency. And there is reason for insecurity. We have mentioned the study of idlers by Downs in an earlier chapter. If the idea is extended to corporations, a survey a year or so ago revealed that the number of executives varied from 12 to 212 per $100 million in sales.[3] One may question both ends of the scale. It is essential to have enough personnel to control the organization but when the average number of executive staff is 46 people per $1 million of sales, it is obvious some organizations have more fat than others. As a real extreme, a large corporation, IC Industries, runs a $4.4 billion a year corporation with 155 people.[3]

Because of these ideas corporations are changing their attitudes toward executive staffs. They are beginning to have only enough staff to provide necessary service; the staff cost is charged directly to the user and when it is not used, the staff is reduced. Purchasing efforts are redirected to get the least cost by buying services when they are cheaper than inhouse efforts. [4]

We are beginning to find that prevalent standards of excellence are not adequate. In the executive ranks, pay and productivity are not related (see Chapter 3), and the performance of the executive is not evaluated in terms of return on investment to the company. We have not measured the objectives of the manager in terms of the needs of the company. In fact, in many cases, high productivity is feared because a demonstration of efficiency may result in a reduction of staff or demonstrate the objectives may be foggy.

All this leads us to the discussion of how to improve productivity. We will assume the organization has taken the usual steps described in most business textbooks of providing workers with Maslow's satisficing attributes, providing the tools for work, and the usual personnel services. We will instead concentrate on how to improve executive performance. There are two major approaches.

The traditional approach to improving productivity for the blue-collar worker and the executive is to sight specific targets of priority in the order of things, and stress efficiency of operation. A newer and better-suited approach is to determine the mission of the organization and measure its capability, design tools to obtain goals, and stress effectiveness rather than efficiency. Both require reeducation of the work force including the executives. Such plans may require several steps:

1. Diagnosis through clarification of aims of service and output. Definition of desired output including user needs and expectations, and identification of the leverage points in the organization where change can be initiated.

2. Determination of objectives through clarification of the exact mission of the organization, and design of a plan to achieve the mission. The plan must be quantitative and specific. It is not sufficient, for example, to say we will increase sales by x millions. The x millions must be broken down into y units and z products in a w time frame.

3. Measurements must be devised to determine if objectives are being met. A time frame for measurement must be devised and perhaps a PERT diagram or similar time-activity chart set up to measure progress.

4. Determination of services needed in order for the executive to fulfill the goals of an organization must be provided. There have been many suggestions that too many services are provided and the executive may well function better with fewer or less costly appurtenances.

5. Need for technology that nowadays may well be the kind of communication equipment needed to support the executive.

Technology should be tailored to the needs of the exact objectives specified.

    6. The organization of a team to implement the plans of the organization.[5]

Obviously the formulations of objectives, plans, and strategies are designed to improve the performance of the executive. This means the executive must change attitude from the American monochronatic type (Chapter 3) to more of the Japanese polychronatic manner. The executive must learn to work in teams instead of alone and must realize that team formation requires a whole new brand of management. The team, in order to function efficiently, must have openness, timeliness in information flow, openmindedness for new ideas, cooperation between members, analytical ability, clear focus of activity, and quick responsiveness. These are not typical characteristics of American business.

GROUP THEORY

All of these responses are rooted in group theory. The Japanese have exploited group theory to the extreme, and American organizations must also begin to approach the problem of managing employees in groups rather than as single individuals. Any organization tends to form formal or informal groups. Groups may be formed to accomplish a task, for gain, for personal satisfaction, to earn esteem of fellow members, for formation of new ideas, for a sense of belonging, or for ego. Groups tend to influence the kind and amount of work done and thus force norms on their members. Such norms may be good or bad. When Frank Gilbreth found a new method of masonry enabling a man to lay three times as many bricks as before, the union intervened to limit the number of bricks laid per day. On the other hand, the Japanese quality circle has resulted in higher norms of performance, in both quality and quantity.

    Groups form by a clearly defined process. The group must develop an acceptance of each member, clearly define a leader, determine means of decision making, develop motivation as a group, and then establish norms of operations. Groups are often in conflict within an organization. The available resources, different goals, a failure to define tasks clearly, and a false perception of goals may lead to conflict within the group and between groups.

    A group has some advantages. It pools resources and knowledge, divides responsibility, provides communication and coordination, and may provide more diverse inputs to a solution. There are also disadvantages: blame is hard to assess, action may be avoided, misallocation of resources may occur, and most decisions are averages representing the sum of diverse views.

    Organizations have often set up group operations without considering the pros and cons of the method. When groups work well, they are highly successful. One Japanese company claims to have received 110,000 new ideas in one

year for improving manufacturing from the quality circles in the plant.
  Group formation usually has several important steps:

1. A clear set of directions must be given for tasks.
2. A strong chairman must be appointed or the group must chose a strong chairman.
3. Staff support must be available.
4. Members must be chosen for ability to address the problem at hand.
5. Membership must be small.
6. Time for decisions must be provided. Consensus must be reached.
7. Groups must be told if their work is supervisory or advisory and the distinction clearly marked.

Achievement of group goals should be the focus of attention for American business. The Japanese ordinarily act in groups and by a group decision, and this requires time that Americans have not been willing to take.

EXECUTIVE TRAINING

Another method of changing executives and their relationship to the group is to change their entire outlook. Several companies specialize in training through techniques involving learning a new business language, learning a new theoretical approach to problems, all mixed with some form of brainwashing, or Eastern mysticism. A new language is forced upon trainees so they learn a new method of using definitions. "The functioning capability of a task cycle" simply means the job description, but the new term is imbued with mystic powers, and the leadership is forced into a cult very little different in methodology from the Hari Krishnas.
  Some executives are now beginning to question the worthwhile outcomes of such procedures. Many now believe that the apparent improvement in executive skills comes not from the training, but from the novelty of the situation. We must remember that the Hawthorne experiment proved many years ago any change in the environment would temporarily improve performance. Even a change in light intensity, whether up or down, would cause a novelty response, and many now believe the new training techniques fall in this category. Kron, Trice, and others have commanded large sums for executive training sessions and there is considerable question as to their value. Pacific Bell spent $40 million on such programs and stated that they consider the process a total waste. Other companies claim that such training works for about 10 percent of workers in each class session and the rest either do not benefit or may actually be distracted from previous levels of work. In other cases, the trainees have expressed total

dissatisfaction with the process and discounted any benefit. The whole process may be no different from the last fads in business— transactional analysis, and S-groups—which disappeared in the same way that this fad will vanish.

As a bad example of the gobbledegook of this genre we can quote from a published article:

> Work in that focus, perceptibility, continuity, and recurrence are primary as-
> pects of concern and organization. These aspects become not only increasingly
> expressive but syntactical in nature. There is a concern for establishing a clear
> focus despite involved schemes of recurrence based on additive or subtractive
> procedures.

We defy anyone to determine the meaning of this statement.

To sum up briefly, changes in the international and national scenes force the creation of a new type of executive.   *U. S. News and World Report* of March 7, 1988, reported that the new manager must become a *global strategist* because last year thousands of trades or corporate mergers were made on the international scene. Unfortunately, executives do not see the international scene as the way to advancement. The manager must also be a *master of technology* because all business today demands computer literacy at the very least. With manufacturing turning to robotics and CAD/CAM procedures, a knowledge of technology is imperative. Executives must become *politicians* because they must operate in a field of government regulations, of competition between governments to expand or limit trade, and all this in ever changing social values, which requires extreme exercise of tact and diplomacy. Finally, they must be *leaders* because the new climate demands reorganization of business and the motivation of workers to new attitudes toward work and quality control.

Again, the same set of problems occurs in academia. Schools of education have traditionally provided a scheme of teaching embedded in the curriculum of all schools of education. The consensus of what would be good to teach, how to improve content, and so on are often neglected or deferred by problems relating to discrimination, selection of students, and other social concerns. Although the book *A Nation at Risk* was published some years ago, there is little concrete ev-idence that the school systems have done anything to improve the situation. The teachers are not a part of the decision-making team and usually the parents are also excluded.

In some respects the government is an example of too much group theory. The formation of committees of inquiry, committees of study, committees of re-view, are all too commonplace, but a committee of decision making has yet to be formed. A typical example is the Packard committee, which years ago report-ed on the possibility of saving billions of dollars in defense funds by tighter or-ganization, objective planning, and better operations. It provided specific exam-ples of steps to be taken; most have not been implemented. We must make a commitment to a tighter control of all phases of our society, not by restrictive laws, but by adopting the rules of good management.

REFERENCES

1.   C. J. Grayson, Jr., and C. O'dell, *American Business, A Two-Minute Warning*. New York: Free Press, 1988.

2.   White House, *Conference on Productivity*. Washington, D.C.: U.S. Government Printing Office, 1987.

3.   S. Ramo, *The Business of Science*. New York: Hill and Wang, 1988.

4.   B. Brophy and M. Walsh, "The 'Just in Time' Worker," *U.S. News and World Report*, November 23, 1987, p. 45.

5.   W. J. Sonnenstuhl and H. M. Trice, *Strategies for Employee Assistance Programs*. Ithaca, N.Y.: ILR Press, 1986.

14

Changing the Cut of the White Collar

As we have previously reported, predictions are that 90 percent of the work force could be white-collar employees by the year 2000. Although there will be general growth in the service industries, the most rapid growth is expected to be in the general areas of paralegal personnel, computer specialists, and medical assistants of several kinds. The Hudson Institute forecasts 3.8 million new management jobs, 5.8 million new professional and technical positions, and 3.6 million new marketing and sales opportunities. In addition, there will be 95 percent more lawyers and judges, which may be good from the standpoint of punishment of the criminal but bad from the standpoint of unnecessary litigation which decreases the GNP. At the same time there will be 400,000 fewer jobs in production.[1]

The Bureau of Labor Statistics (BLS) estimates that 55 percent of all employees are now in white-collar positions. And strangely enough, with the rise of high technology and the use of computers in manufacturing, 30 percent of all production jobs are white-collar in nature. And as computer control, CAD/CAM production, and robots increase in number, the white-collar employees in production will likely increase further.

The productivity growth rate in the service industries is stagnant and may be decreasing, and that sector accounts for two-thirds of all private production output in the United states. As we have remarked, productivity in the service sector adds little to the economy and may actually cause a decrease in productivity. This is the main reason that it is essential to improve the performance of the white-collar worker, and the main reason that we are not world leaders today. The litigious society in which we live decreases productivity in the economy as a whole as the result of costs of lawyers and cost of judgments.

It is important to note that some companies have awakened to the decreased productivity and are doing something about it. We will discuss a few example of efforts made by companies to improve productivity. The descriptions are generic because each company is an individual and programs must be tailored to the company needs.

STUDIES IN PRODUCTIVITY

A landmark study of worker productivity was conducted by the American Productivity and Quality Center of Houston and published as *White Collar Productivity: The National Challenge.*[2] In the study, questionnaires were mailed to 600 major firms. The questionnaire contained a series of questions concerning white-collar performance and the steps taken by each company to improve performance in the workplace. Almost one-half the recipients stated that they had no clear objectives for improvement. This is almost unbelievable in an era of decreasing productivity and decreasing profits.

The study did show that managers thought that savings could potentially be very great if improvements were implemented; that little was being done by industry to change from the present methods of production; that the added value of white-collar work is usually overlooked; and that improvement occurs spasmodically, lacks integration, and emerges haphazardly from the executive suite. At the same time senior management endorsed the need for improvement, indicating a dichotomy of purpose and direction. Middle-level management appeared to be totally left out of all discussions and contributed nothing to the results of the company studies even though it has been clearly demonstrated in Japan that the middle-level manager is often the determining factor in improving productivity. From this level comes a majority of inventions, improvements in processes, and coordination of effort. These results pointed up the defects in the American management system, which were discussed more theoretically above.

Based on the survey, a research project was launched to test several assumptions:

1. Ownership of any improvement effort must be held by the work group involved. They, and not management, are critical to success.

2. Members of the white-collar group must participate actively in the improvement process. Tacit approval is not sufficient to indicate commitment.

3. Traditional approaches must be abandoned in favor of internal changes. Use of outside expertise is not dependable.

4. The group must be ready to adapt quickly to changes in the company or the environment.

5. White-collar productivity must involve a focus on doing the right things as well as doing things right.

6. White-collar groups need to be responsive to clients' or users' needs.

7. Improvement must include both efficiency and effectiveness. It is relatively easy to be efficient but if the efficiency is directed toward the wrong goals, the effectiveness is poor.

8. White-collar groups need to understand why they exist and for what purpose, and how they serve the institution as a whole. Defining service and the customer prompts a white-collar group to look at its organization and find activities that could be changed or eliminated. Services, as opposed to activities, can serve as a useful focus of analysis and evaluation, but the results are often not satisfactory because the white-collar group does not have a product that can be easily measured. Services are less context specific and more functionally independent.

9. A group must look beyond its own parochial boundaries and consider its impact on the organization as a whole.

10. Any effort must be based in the organization itself. Focus on the internal customer is critical to the external customer's approval.

11. Productivity improvement must address both technical and social issues. As the Japanese have found, addressing technical issues alone may streamline procedures but fail to address the working relationships which are more critical. On the other hand, attacking only the social issues may improve communications but not improve productivity.

These assumptions, confirmed by the survey, focused attention on the objectives of productivity improvement and sparked interest in a number of companies that had taken steps to improve performance. We will discuss several case histories later.

AREAS OF PRODUCTIVITY IMPROVEMENT

Several studies have suggested that the worker is capable of identifying areas for improvement. As an example, workers in an audit group have suggested increasing the measures for productivity, more emphasis on where and when decisions are made, better communications between all levels in the organization, and automation of functions and better training programs in use of automated processes. An operations group suggested better clerical staff and better career ladders. A group in customer service found need for better plant environment including studies on computer fatigue, noise, and temperature changes. An accounting group identified needed equipment, more telephone contacts, and improved communications.

Notice that the range of ideas for increasing productivity is very wide and that it is different from area to area, encompassing virtually all of white-collar activity.

MEASUREMENT OF PRODUCTIVITY

The survey mentioned above suggested that failure to measure objectives was a real obstacle to determination of performance of white-collar workers. Their output cannot be calculated in terms of units per hour, sales per day, or other such factors and the white-collar worker typically has more discretion on the job than other workers. This creates difficulty in measurement.

Unfortunately, this state of affairs has led to the situation where one or two parameters are used to evaluate the white-collar worker, and many of these may be irrelevant. Measuring "tons of steel per hour of typing" is not likely to yield beneficial results for evaluating such workers. The traditional measurements of productivity must be scrapped in favor of a different approach:

1. Service as a whole must be measured rather than evaluating simple activities.

2. A comprehensive group of measures must be established.

3. Employees in the work group must establish measures rather than an outside group.

4. Measures must be for an entire group, not an individual.

5. Measures must be designed to plan and train rather than to control and monitor.

6. Effectiveness as well as efficiency must be measured. While organizations must be involved, the internal customer must be pleased first and will be first to judge the performance.

Effectiveness measurements must also be used to make judgments about the output versus outcome of the group. The sheer volume of output is not a good measure if the quality is low, because then quality control and rejection of finished goods will mean that the total outcome is poor. But it is possible to initiate measures successfully in groups. Without such ideas for effectiveness, the group cannot find problems, make corrections, and improve performance.

We have mentioned that the computer provides vast amounts of information and is often used as a measure of change. But information alone does not make change unless the information is used to make corrections, modify the work process, or redirect work efforts. In the long run the establishment of standards is critical. In addition, a plan for implementation of comparison of actual work against standards must be carefully devised. The group with real desires to make improvements never matches its work against a given measurement with the idea of punishment or the holding up of goals. The idea of creating a measurement system is to educate, not to punish.

EXAMPLES OF IMPROVEMENT EFFORTS

The following are a few examples of work groups that have implemented improvements and produced tangible results. [2] Details of actual goals and measurements are not included, as each changes with particular circumstances, and each group must devise its own standards and measure its own success. In each case a different type of company using a different method has been identified.

Insurance Company

Background. A major insurance company had increasing price competition in the property and casualty insurance fields. A basic strategy was needed to improve performance so that costs would remain at present levels.

Action. An assessment revealed redundancy of effort between departments suggesting that: consolidation was necessary and that authority levels needed to be reevaluated and shifted; operations needed to be streamlined. Better counseling and career planning was needed, and award and recognition procedures needed to be enhanced. Training needed to be expanded and better use of technology developed in a computer environment. An action plan was devised to correct all of the listed deficiencies. The plan was adopted.

Results. Annual savings totaled more than $5 million per year including $3.4 million in organizational changes as a result of personnel shift; $1 million was saved by elimination of outside services through employee training, and $900,000 was saved in process changes through the use of new technology.

Human Resources Group

Background. A human resource group in the aerospace industry controlled employment, compensation, relocation, and benefits of all employees in a large company. The department wanted to provide training for employees, enhance staff courtesy, and introduce better system operations. There were long delays in notification of employees regarding changes in status, hiring or termination that needed to be changed. In addition, no personnel were aware of personnel procedures, contract labor was necessary to handle the work load, and access to employee information was difficult.

Action Taken. A computerized data base was implemented to control personnel files. Regular staff meetings of employees were introduced to review policy and resolve questions of personnel management. A second shift of clerks was added to decrease waiting time and improve records.

Results. Immediate results were an annual saving of $130,000. A new document control system eliminated much paperwork, permitted access to files, and saved $25,000 in annual costs.

Consumer Services

Background. The Reporting Department provided business information reports to other departments in the company and to outside subscribers. Employee turnover ranged as high as 100 percent per year, costing the company about $10,000 per person (as high as $350,000 per year). There were large backlogs of output. The goals were to reduce personnel turnover, improve response to customers, improve morale, and improve communications.

Action Taken. A incentive plan was devised to reward prompt response, accuracy of reports, and attitude toward customers. Changes in the salary structure resulted in a more desirable place to work. The staff was encouraged to provide input into problem solutions.

Results. Employee turnover dropped dramatically to less than 10 percent per year. Response time to customers decreased. A 50 percent drop in the backlog was achieved and the quality of work improved by almost 10 percent. By addressing only the soft issues such as morale, participation, and communications, dramatic results in the bottom line were achieved.

Management Information Systems

Background. A information resource group in a large electrical utility provided programming support and engineering solutions (CAD/CAM) to engineering departments. There was a lack of communications, decreased response due to paperwork load, and poor personnel skills.

Actions Taken. A task force was set up in the group. It established a computer mail capability, reduced typed forms for intergroup communication, and established a mentor program to teach new employees the policies and procedures in the department. Single contact points were established between the group members and correspondents. These groups were then divided into separate subgroups, each of which handled specific customers to maintain contact during absences of the normal contact person.

Results. Implementation of better paper flow, a system of training, and improvement in response time resulted in a saving of $60,000, the equivalent of two employees.

Personnel

Background. The personnel department of an aerospace company maintains and stores documents relating to employment including access to all employment in the company. Paperwork was initiated at the department level, and after review and approval went to personnel where clerks entered the data in the data base after checks for accuracy. Access to current data was critical, but was not available because of the way the department handled payroll and personnel actions.

Action Taken. Work was redesigned to produce a system for handling rapid updates to the records system. Departments now enter data directly into the data system where it is stored in a buffer file and reviewed automatically for exceptions to rules and then entered into the data base. Exceptions are handled manually by personnel.

Results. The system now avoids double entry of data, provides departmental access to personnel files and reduces error. Incidentally, no new computer facilities were needed. The department is now saving about $1 million per year.

Customer Service

Background. A circulation department in a customer service company ensures that subscriptions are delivered on time, maintains subscriber data bases, provides toll free telephone service for inquiries, and makes changes in addresses and subscriptions. The department had a large volume of work in replacement publications and answering customer complaints. All services were poor.

Action Taken: The work group identified four major inhibitors to work flow: unnecessary management approvals which slowed operations, ineffective use of resources due to lack of cross-training between disciplines, no standard procedures, which inhibited cross-training and caused quality errors, and lack of focus on the customer.
Suggestions to remove inhibitions were implemented. Management approvals were reduced, procedures were documented, traineeship was encouraged, employees solicited customers about service needs, a "postal watch" program was begun with the Post Office to trace missing documents, and related changes were made, including automating routine activities.

Results. Telephone surveys indicate that customer satisfaction has markedly improved. Replacement orders were reduced 47 percent, and a total of more than $125,000 annual savings were achieved. In addition, overtime and staffing requirements were sharply reduced.

Finance and Accounting/Engineering

Background.   A defense contract company analyzes and interprets financial and scheduling data for use by senior management and the Department of Defense in tracking the status of projects and governmental contracts. The major output is a Variance Analysis Report (VAR) explaining the changes in contracts and why a contract is over or under budget. The data is handled by two groups: an engineering group needed to explain the overrun or scheduling problem, and a financial group responsible for reporting VARs.

Action Taken.   The average time to process a VAR was two weeks, and the average rejection rate by senior management was 50 percent because of missing information or inadequate explanations. The VAR was placed on a word processor in a single format to permit easy changes. A weekly meeting of engineers and financial personnel was scheduled to review each week's VARs, suggest changes, and agree on the final form. The VARs were made accessible on the computer system to everyone.

Results.   The quality of the VARs improved dramatically. The rejection rate fell from 50 percent to about 12.5 percent and the time of review fell from two weeks to one day. The staff reported feeling like a part of the organization rather than like glorified clerks shuffling papers.

THE WHITE-COLLAR WORKPLACE

The white-collar work force faces a difficult, challenging environment.[2]   The economic climate is in constant flux. Organizations of today are unstable, forced to change products and services under the strain of increasing foreign competition, regulation or deregulation of industries, and a wave of mergers and acquisitions.

Companies have completely changed their corporate persona. Singer no longer makes sewing machines, Greyhound no longer has bus routes as the major source of income, and U.S. Steel no longer considers steel as a major item in its inventory. Hundreds of other examples could be cited. The modern conglomerate handles hundreds of products. Managers of such operations are in a quandary. On the one hand they are likely to be financial experts, trained in business administration, but they may be forced to deal with highly technical developments for which they have no training. The problem of the American executive is apparent. In Chapter 5 we have pointed out the way the Japanese manager is trained to know every part of the company and how it functions. The American executive must change to a similar attitude.

The changes are more complicated and more difficult for the white-collar worker than for a blue-collar counterpart. The worker on an assembly line always has the tangible evidence of what the employer does because it is seen in the daily output, while the white-collar worker deals in more abstract items and the corporate objectives may be much less clear. R and D personnel may be the one example of white-collar workers who have a sense of mission. For the accountants, management information systems (MIS) workers, and other similar employees, there is no clear connection between daily tasks and corporate objectives. These persons are often more loyal to their profession than to the business. This may explain in part the ready movement of personnel from one job to another. This does not occur in those countries (again notably Japan) where a major corporate objective is an instillation of company loyalty through lifetime employment, benefits, and a family approach.

Professional loyalty as opposed to organizational loyalty makes a good deal of sense in modern America. Downsizing and mergers interrupt careers. Career development in many corporations is nonexistent. In a recent survey, only 26 percent of managers said they had a clear idea of the career opportunities and ladders in their workplace. The chances of a twenty-five-year career with one employer are almost nonexistent. CEOs move on the average every three years, which discourages attempts at company loyalty. Thus, if one cannot be a lifelong employee, one can be a lifelong accountant or computer specialist.[3]

There is a positive side to this professional employee attitude. White-collar workers usually believe that they have high performance standards and are encouraged to high performance by managers in the same profession. It behooves the CEO to devise methods by which this desire for high-level performance can be channeled into better productivity for the organization as a whole.

LEADERSHIP

The basic failure of organization to obtain good productivity can be summed up in one word—leadership. Leadership has been missing in the CEOs of American corporations. Attention is focused upon profits, return to stockholders, and individual salaries. Little attention has been paid to the factors that will increase productivity.[4] We have already quoted Lee Iacocca: "I can make more money for Chrysler managing money than making cars." Productivity is often interpreted by these money managers as a speedup of the work force. This is not a unique attitude. It is an attitude which discourages quality, and, as we have seen, speeding up of productivity in terms of units per hour without the requisite increase in quality is a waste of time.

A good (poor) example of mismanagement is the way technology is handled in modern corporations. The average CEO does not understand technology and does not press for its productive use. As a result, many white-collar workers feel technology is available to them, is adequate for the job, but is unused. At one time everyone expected the desktop terminal or computer to solve management problem, but as we have mentioned (Chapter 6), the underuse of computers and the overaccessibility of elaborate data bases may have actually decreased productivity. In addition, the tendency in large corporations is to lock up computers, give command to the MIS department, and make the computers inaccessible to the white-collar employee who could make good use of the potential. CEOs have not made attempts to train employees, make them familiar with computers, and encourage use of the machines. As a result, many corporations have hundreds of computers with a utilization rate of almost zero. Until the CEO forces himself and other top mangers to actually use the computers on their desk tops, the situation will not change.

REFERENCES

1.   American Productivity and Quality Center, *Impact One: The White Collar Work Force.* Houston, Tex.: American Productivity and Quality Center, 1988.

2.   American Productivity and Quality Center, *The White Collar Productivity — A National Challenge.* Houston, Tex.: American Productivity and Quality Center, 1988.

3.   "At the Top," *Competition Flash,* American Management Association, New York, July 1990, p. 48.

4.   American Productivity and Quality Center, *An Example of Japanese Total Quality Control.* Houston, Tex.: American Productivity and Quality Center, 1989.

15

Developing a Mindset Toward Quality

As a nation we have ignored quality. The definition of quality control and its implementation in Japan were initiated by an American, W. Deming, after neglect by manufacturers in the United States. There is no question but that his ideas have made Japan the quality leader and forced American businesses into a secondary position.[1] The American idea of quality is not to build it into manufacturing but to control the quality by inspection after the fact. Quality has not been pushed into manufacturing.

American factories tend to accept the lowest bidder in production material. Japan has traditionally taken a few subcontractors, encouraged quality, and purchased from them. In addition, they have added the concept of concurrent engineering, frequent changes, and inspection at the group level. We have expected management to legislate quality into products, and this is clearly impossible. Quality must begin at the grass roots with a total commitment. American CEOs have not exhibited the leadership necessary to implement this great change in our organizations.

Japanese total quality control (TQC) has been a threatening move in the United States. There have been a few moves to implement TQC in our system, but there have been more failures than successes. And as we move to TQC, the Japanese are one step ahead with total control (TC). The work in "fuzzy logic" and large CAD/CAM systems are allowing the Japanese to lead the world.[2]

The Japanese system is simple. Control rests on people and machines. The control is vested in a "machine keeper" responsible for the machine and its operations. The machine operator may be a lower paid employee. The keeper is expected to:

1. Have a thorough understanding of the process.
2. Accept responsibility for meeting goals.
3. Perform routine maintenance.

4. Monitor function and evaluate results.
5. Solve most problems independently.
6. Be able to call for assistance when needed.

TQC is based on a series of principles which apply in any situation, including training and motivation of the work force, which is the moving factor, tolerating only the best materials, using manufacturable designs modified as necessary and as often as needed, and tight control of process and equipment to maximize operational traits.

This commitment has led Japan to dominate the computer chip market, the manufacture and use of robots, and the "just in time" manufacturing concept.

We may ask if the TQC will work in the American workplace. Will our workers adopt this practice? If the concept is adopted, can it endure if the total organization is not changed? There are no clear answers but it is true that some changes are occurring.[3]   A few early pioneers have attempted to implement TQC with some success. A few examples include the following.

1. Federal Express has a concept taught to all employees, Q=P, quality equals productivity. They have created an atmosphere that takes fear out of change. A management institute trains managers to operate in the new mode.

2. Averitt Express has set up five standards, which are the hallmark of the company. They are excellence in hiring and training personnel, effective approaches to communication with employees where everyone is an "associate," measuring and monitoring productivity at all levels, placing significant emphasis on customer services, and conducting effective safety programs.

3. The Naval Air Research Facility, San Diego, is a total quality effort aimed at a single consumer, the United States Fleet. The top management has been trained in the Deming philosophy and includes steering committees, process action teams, and quality management boards. Both statistical analysis and quality circles are used to attain the quality effort.

4. General Technology (GTE) and people are interwoven at GTE. The Interactive Computer Graphics Program (ICGS) is used to unite the entire operation for work mapping and record keeping. Employee Quality Involvement Proces (EQUIP) insures that all employees have training, knowledge and skills to analyze business processes and make recommendations for improvement. The third part of the quality program is the Employee Participation Process (EPP), intended to create an informed and individualized employee participating in all elements of the company operation.

5. Avis Rent-A-Car sees quality as its competitive edge. There is a

quantitative measurement program, which has restructured service standards and led to a complete reorganization of the Avis management structure.

    6. Cigna has set internal standards of service access, effectiveness of communications, and administration as a result of surveys of customer attitudes.

    7. ARA Services has a "spirit of service" which is taught to every employee.

These are only a few examples of attempts by companies to address service quality. Again the message is clear, each company must address its own problems and its own solutions. There is no general universal solution.

Paying attention to quality has developed into a crusade for the few who believe that America lags behind the rest of the developed world in quality and that quality could be improved. The White House Conference on Productivity, published in April 1984, put the matter bluntly:

> America is the most productive nation on earth but its growth in productivity has faltered. Some of the factors contributing to slower productivity growth are within our control and some are not, but it is important that we respond to this challenge.

Many national leaders in business and business organizations launched quality improvement programs as a result. The National Advisory Council on Quality (NASQ), the American Society for Quality Control (ACQC), the American Productivity and Quality Center (APQC), and the National Productivity Advisory Committee (NPAC) all began to develop ideas that led to legislation. The furor followed by some years the creation of the Japanese Union of Scientists and Engineers (JUSE), which had first advocated quality control.

All efforts culminated in the Malcolm Baldridge National Quality Improvement Act signed into law by President Ronald Reagan on August 20, 1987. [3] The act is a part of a national effort to improve the quality of goods and services in the United States and demonstrates the growing cooperation of business and government to achieve this goal. The act listed several purposes and findings:

    1. Leadership of the United States in product and process quality has been strongly challenged by foreign competitors.

    2. Productivity growth has decreased in relation to our competitors over the last two decades.

    3. Failure to alter this trend will lead to a lower standard of living and less opportunity for Americans.

    4. Japan in 1985 became the world's top creditor nation while the

United States became the largest net debtor nation.

5. In Japan the JUSE sponsors the Deming Award for national quality improvement, which is a strong incentive to Japanese comanies.

6. American industry is beginning to understand that improved quality of goods and service goes hand in hand with improved productivity.

7. The bill should help stimulate American companies to improve quality and productivity or the pride of recognition and to maintain a competitive edge through increased profits.

8. The act provides mechanisms to recognize the achievements of those companies that improve quality of their goods and provide an example to others, establishes guidelines and criteria that can be used by business, industry, and government in evaluating their own quality improvement efforts, and provides specific guidelines for American enterprises that wish to learn to manage for high quality.

In order to provide adequate reward for improving quality and productivity, a medal, the Malcolm Baldridge Award, is presented by the White House annually to the most improved organization. The details are provided in Appendix A.

REFERENCES

1.   W. E. Deming, *Sample Design in Business Research.* New York: John Wiley and Sons, 1960.

2.   K. Self, "Designing with Fuzzy Logic," *IEEE Spectrum* 27 (11):42 (November 1990).

3.   American Productivity and Quality Center, *An Example of Japanese Total Quality Control.* Houston, Tex.: American Productivity and Quality Center, 1989.

16

What's a Manager to Do?

Bombarded from all sides, an executive lives on a precipice in today's world. Each day brings conflicting demands from consumers, owners, stockholders, personnel, government(s), and the community. Unfortunately, most of those presently occupying the executive suite are from the old school of business and training by "hard knocks," schooled in the management techniques of Maslow and others, to direct, organize, and control operations; they are not equipped to handle the pressures of modern business. Sadly, the line of succession contains many of the same ilk. Hopefully, their successors will be the last of this genre.

Unfortunately, but truthfully, performance of an executive is measured solely by his impact on the bottom line; the return to the stockholder. The stockholder, and often the board member, expects large, short-term gains. Little attention is paid to the long-term objectives of the corporation. In addition, the executive often has a hand in the pie; quick profits lead to quick raises and stock options. In July 1990 a report from the American Management Association said, "In 1989, the CEO salary increase outstripped the profits in many companies."

An analysis of the top one hundred industrial concerns in the United States found that a median increase in the compensation of the CEO was about 9 percent while company profit increases averaged about 5 percent. The top compensation of American executives averaged $550,000, while in Japan the average top compensation was about $350,000. And we must remember that the Japanese business man was a better manager and produced a higher quality product.

The American CEO has other problems. The consumer finds faults with the average corporation. Business indicators and consumer surveys suggest that public reaction is negative. The state of the economy is poor, and this can be traced directly to the American manager and his methods. The white-collar worker is aware of the deficiencies and understands the relationship between quality production and financial success but is not allowed to implement his ideas. The blue-collar worker has never been encouraged to have any part in company planning and as a result does not care about quality and is concerned only about individual direct income.

A good example is in the automobile industry. Workers have been discouraged from suggestions, encouraged to work in an assembly-line mode, and, as a result, the Japanese auto makers whose workers enter into the decision process may dominate the industry with a 40 percent share by the year 2000. A large part of the market will be dominated by Toyota, Nissan, and Honda because these companies make better cars twice as fast as American plants, and the consumer is well aware of the facts. In addition, the repair record of American cars is dismal, while that of the Japanese is superb. And this is the fault of American managers.

And the problem is not only in manufacturing. Services have a dismal record as well. The Japanese (again) are acquiring the 10 largest banks in the United States while they already own four of the largest banks in the world. In just five years international banking has increased from 21 to 40 percent of trade in Japan while it has declined from 27 to 15 percent in the United States. American business complains that Japan has money to buy industries, banks, and real estate, but they fail to explain that the money came in the first place from better management and productivity.

CEOs complain about government regulation and its effect on the stultification of American business and the bottom line. The reverse situation may be more correct. Better quality products, attention to consumer demands, and similar steps might well reduce the need for regulation. Would the auto companies have voluntarily reduced emissions without the threat of government subvention? We doubt it. Would the Exxon disaster, the junk bond affair, and failure of the savings and loan organizations have been prevented by more regulation? We believe it would. There has been much complaint about the overregulation of the nuclear power industry, resulting in its virtual demise. If we built and operated plants with the efficiency of the Japanese, the British, or the French, regulations would not be so important. Again the managers should be blamed.

In another vein, regulatory action is cited as the evidence of poor government decision making, but in the present situation there is every indication that the government is making better decisions than the corporate executives. We should adopt the old political slogan, "Throw the rascals out."

Almost every company making products or providing services is facing an avalanche of consumer dissatisfaction. There are complaints of shoddy workmanship, many returns for repairs, and a poor attitude toward the consumer. As one example, auto makers have announced that they will provide air bags for driver protection in all cars by 1992, although the technology has been available for years and is a definite safety measure. Antilock brakes are just now available, usually at extra cost. American cars still have thirty-year-old engines, while newer foreign cars have four ports per cylinder and smaller, more efficient drives. Ralph Nader has been accused of being the gadfly for American industry, but if the industry performed as it should, Nader would be out of business.

And dissatisfaction is not only on the part of the consumer. Employee dissatisfaction is a major problem for the executive. The happy worker is essential for quality production and high productivity, and in today's job market of declining employee loyalty, decreased morale, poor training, and evaporating markets, the CEO is hard pressed. In addition, the worker is pressing for a say in management. As the idea of the Quality Circle and the Z-style of management becomes more widely known, the employees demand a greater share in the decision making. This can be an advantage if the end result is better quality and greater employee loyalty, but all too often the reasons are to pressure the corporation for greater benefits.

What's a manager to do?

THE GOOD LISTENER

Some executives are good listeners. They keep an ear to the voices of the market, the customers, the stockholders, and the employees. But they are a new breed. Mike Barlow, in an article in the *Houston Chronicle* of October 29, 1989, pointed out the present situation very well. Barlow makes the point that the executive is changing his stripes. The autocrats, tyrants, and eyegougers are a vanishing breed. He is backed up by G.B. Harvey, the president of Pitney-Bowe, who said, "The old style won't work here. The employees would throw you out." Another CEO remarked, "The only way a CEO can be an S.O.B. is to own 51 percent of the business." Yet A. Neuharth, in his book on executives entitled *Confessions of an S.O.B.,* says the modern executive must be another Ghengis Khan to survive. [1] The dichotomy is clear, and it does not bode well for American business.

It is difficult to set standards for business. The "man in the gray flannel suit" has almost disappeared. The "twentieth floor" syndrome is still here, but it is being eroded by the Japanese invasion of American business. The modern executive must learn to be closer to the employees. There must be an attitude of forthrightness and honesty in a day when the employee is gaining power steadily. A new skill in handling people is essential.

The CEO is also faced with a more knowledgeable clientele. While it is true that the knowledge may come from the television screen with all its biases, the CEO must be prepared to respond to demands and complaints. Lee Iacocca, Victor Kiam, and Frank Lorenzo are CEOs who have gotten the message and appear regularly on television, selling their companies and their products.

Forbes Magazine of May 28, 1989, listed twenty-five of the best CEOs in the country. It is not practical to review the list, but it is interesting to observe the styles adopted by most of the group. One of the main ideas is the response to the consumer. Most executives remarked that it was essential to listen to the customers as they asked for new products or discarded old ones.

WHAT IS LEADERSHIP?

Are leadership and management the same? To manage means to bring about, to accomplish, to have responsibility for results. It is the ability to achieve work through people, and this requires motivation. Motivation occurs, according to business theory, through one of two processes. There are X-type managers who believe that people dislike work and avoid it. As a result this type of manager controls and directs employees. The Y-type manager, on the other hand, believes that people like to work, seek responsibility, and work creatively. This manager provides direction (not directing), training, and motivation. This approach requires that the CEO become a guide, an influencing factor, and an opinion former, rather than an autocrat.[2]

The styles can be separated into three modes:[3]

Authoritarian: The leader determines policy, techniques, and activities, and is "personal" in attitude for praise or blame.

Democratic: A group makes decisions on policy, establishes goals, and organizes as needed, while the group leader is fact-minded in praise or blame.

Laissez-faire: Minimum participation of leader who offers only information and materials, and does not attempt to regulate the course of events.

The first and third cases are unlikely to succeed in the modern world; the second case is illustrated by the quality circle, which has been demonstrated to work.

The general theses of leadership have been summarized by Bennis Warren and Nannus in their book *Leaders*, identifying four strategies for leadership.[4]

Strategy 1: *Attention through vision*. Leadership is a transaction between leaders and followers. The leader must create a vision of where the goals are and how to reach them.

Strategy 2: *Meaning through communication*. The leader must realize that nothing can be accomplished without adequate communication. To obtain acceptance of a new idea, the employees must be attracted, and their attention caught at every level of the operation.

Strategy 3: *Trust through positioning*. The leader must make a clear demonstration of trust in and reliance upon the employees. Exhortation will not work. Trust is also implied by a constancy of direction and aims. In order to achieve the aims of the corporation and create innovation, the executive must be prepared to iterate and reiterate new ideas,which also indicates leadership positioning.

Strategy 4: *Deployment of self through self-regard and the Wallenda factor.* Self-regard of the leader must be developed through a knowledge of strengths and weaknesses. Compensatory measures for weakness must be taken through staff organization and new expertise. The self-regard must be strong enough that the executive can deal with situations for which there is no expertise. This means that executives must have a good knowledge of their own strengths and weaknesses, have the capacity to find and nurture strength in others to implement the missing factors, and have the ability to determine the fit between the persona of the executive and the needs of the organization.

Warren and Nanus found that five key skills were necessary to implement these major premises:

1. The ability to accept people as they are and work with the available material.
2. The capacity to approach problems as they exist today rather than to look for yesterday's solution.
3. The ability to treat those close to one in the same manner as strangers would be treated in order to hear useful information, which might be discarded from one too near.
4. The ability to trust others although the risk is great.
5. The ability to conduct business as usual without constant approval or recognition.

The Wallenda factor was named after the great aerialist who was unafraid to undertake impossible tasks, to do so under adverse conditions, and to try all alternatives. The acceptance of challenge and the ability to "try" is a great skill in the manager, and is related to self-realization. Self-regard determines the willingness to try to perform a task, and the capability to actually complete it.

WHAT IS QUALITY LEADERSHIP?

O. Harari and Mukai, writing in the *Management Review,* August 1990, listed qualifications which they considered essential for a good executive.[5] They included the ability to be proactive and not reactive, the ability to cause change, and the ability to be a team player. Other characteristics listed are modesty, continued high performance, willingness to accept responsibility, belief in a horizontal management structure, and commitment to quality.

We have mentioned that self-regard creates a sense of self confidence and high expectation in executives, and in those working with them. In addition, a childlike attitude may be helpful. A childlike attitude is often used to deride an executive who uses little technology or modern decision-making techniques in arriving at a decision. However, if childlike is assumed to be the characteristics of enthusiasm, curiosity, spontaneity, imagination, and ability to change rapidly, these suggest a good manager.

Let us end with a final comment. Each of the principles outlined above can be learned by a manager seeking to improve style. And in the final analysis, managers are made—not born.

REFERENCES

1.   A. Neuharth, *Confessions of an S.O.B.* New York: Doubleday, 1989.

2.   J. Hall, *Models for Management: The Structure of Competence.* Woodlands, Tex.: Woodstead Press, 1988.

3.   W. Bennis and B. Nanus, *Leaders.* New York: Harper and Row, 1985.

4.   L. M. Miller, *Barbarians to Bureaucrats.* New York: Clarkson N. Potter, 1989.

5.   O. Harari and L. Mukai, "A New Decade Demands a New Breed of Manager," *Management Review,* August 1990, p. 20.

Appendix

The Japanese Deming Award sponsored by the Japanese Union of Scientists and Engineers (JUSE) has great impact on companies seeking to improve quality and productivity in Japan. As early as 1980, efforts were being made in the United States to create a similar prestigious award. APQC held a series of teleconferences in 1983, and a dominant theme was the need for such an award. In September 1983, the White House Conference on Quality was held, and again the group recommended a prestigious award for outstanding quality improvement to be given by the President. In 1985 a committee to seek a National Quality Award was formed from a group of private-sector academic leaders.

The first matter to be settled was the name of the award. After much discussion of names, the National Quality Award was selected. Corporate leaders donated funds for support of the infrastructure. Florida Power and Light was a leading agent of change, and the White House indicated support. In 1985, a bill was introduced in the House Committee on Science and Technology. Spurred by the tragic death of Malcolm Baldridge in 1987, the award was renamed the Malcolm Baldridge National Quality Award, and legislation was rapidly passed by the Senate and House of Representatives and signed by the President.

The National Institute of Standards and Technology (NIST), formerly the Bureau of Standards, was selected to direct and manage the award program. The legislation called for a Board of Overseers with members noted in the field of quality management to meet annually and review the program.

A foundation for the Malcolm Baldridge National Quality Award was established to secure funds to operate the program. It now has a forty-two member Board of Trustees, including representatives of major United States companies. Every effort is made to assure that no company has a hand in the decision making.

Day-to-day operations are carried out by a consortium of several societies instrumental in quality control research. Awards are made by a Board of Examiners with nine judges, twenty-eight senior and one hundred regular examiners. Each is a quality control expert. The judges were selected with White House approval and they in turn selected the examiners.

Development of criteria for selection was a major task. Seven examination categories were selected after a study of Deming methods, receipt of ideas from leaders in United States industry, and the recommendations of the quality-oriented societies. Although the program will evolve, the seven major items are expected to remain as the foundation of the evaluation scheme. There are forty-four subcategories which may be changed and there are a total of sixty-two examination questions or criteria for applicants to address. All items were subjected to intense feedback before selection.

The selection is based on a detailed application, a site visit to the applicant company, and a careful review at three levels. The review is based on a set of eight major criteria.

1. A plan for continuous improvement.
2. A system for measuring the improvements.
3. A strategic plan with benchmarks to compare company performance with the best possible standard.
4. A close partnership with suppliers and customers feeding back improvements.
5. Understanding of customers to translate wants into products.
6. A long-lasting relationship with customers to include sales, service, and maintenance.
7. Focus on preventing mistakes rather than correcting them.
8. A total commitment by the entire organization to quality improvement.

In the first year, sixty-six companies met all criteria and were reviewed. Three were selected. In the second year only forty applied, and two met the criteria. The criteria are hard to define and an example of the awards may illustrate the process of selection. Motorola won with a program of total consumer satisfaction, spending $50 million per year on training of the work force, and concentrating on products which were easy to manufacture. Westinghouse had a focus on product development, employee involvement, and consumer satisfaction. A Westinghouse specialty is highly integrated consumer relations. Xerox uses criteria, "Team Xerox" in which quality is integrated into management at all levels. Every employee knows his position and when he is empowered to act. Milliken believes that management should create a vision and provide the environment and the rest will be done by employees.

There have been complaints. The services industries fail to meet the criteria for selection largely because the criteria for measuring services are not well developed. David Snediker of Battelle Institute argues that meeting the criteria forces companies into a mold that is consistent with the aims of the award but may not be consistent with aims of business or profits.[1] The Baldridge Award is a "creeping bureaucracy," he says. Many companies have argued that there is a multitude of standards to choose from in improving quality. Is the Baldridge Award any more definitive than others?

However, industry appears to be coalescing around the Baldridge Award by accepting its standards as a measure of quality. Many companies are using the criteria as internal standards. Others have reported dramatic results from using the criteria. In short the Baldridge Award is a continuously improving tool for raising quality.

REFERENCE

1.   J. Comola, "Malcolm Baldridge Award Winners Display the Human Side of Quality." *Health Care Report* 3:6 (1990).

Bibliography

Aaron, H. J., ed. *Setting National Priorities.* Washington, D.C.: Brookings Institution, 1990.

Aburdene, P. "How to Think like a CEO for the 90's." *Working Woman,* September 1990, p. 134.

Adams, J. L. *Conceptual Blockbusting.* San Francisco: W. H. Freeman, 1974.

American Productivity and Quality Center. *Positioning Corporate Staff for the 1990's.* Houston, Tex.: American Productivity and Quality Center, 1986.

Axelrod, R. *The Evolution of Cooperation.* New York: Basic Books, 1984.

Baig, E. C. "The Great Earnings Gamble." *U.S. News and World Report,* September 17, 1990, p. 65.

Baily, M. N. "Productivity in a Changing World." *Brookings Institution* 18:1 (1981).

Bainbridge, L., and S. A. R. Quintanilla, eds. *Developing Skills with Information Technology.* New York: John Wiley and Sons, 1989.

Becker, H., and D. J. Fritzsche. "Business Ethics." *J. of Business Ethics* 6:289 (1987).

Benchley, P. *Q Clearance.* New York: Random House, 1986.

Bernstein, A. "Help Wanted." *Business Week,* August 10, 1987, p. 48.

Bikson, T. K., and B. A. Gutek. *New Technology in the Office.* New York: Work in America Institute, 1980.

Blake, R. R., and J. S. Mouton, *The Managerial Grid.* Houston, Tex.: Gulf Publishing Co., 1964.

Bloom, B. S., and O. L. Peterson. "End Results, Cost, and Productivity of Coronary-Care Units." *New England J. of Medicine* 288:72 (1973).

Boulding, K. *Conflict and Defense.* New York: Harper and Row, 1962.

Branscomb, L. M. "National and Corporate Technology Strategies in an Interdependent World Economy." *Bridge* 16 (2):8 (Summer 1986).

Brooks, S. "Giving More to the Have Nots." *Insight,* March 27, 1989, p. 28.

Brophy, B., and M. Walsh. "The 'Just in Time' Worker." *U.S. News and World Report,* November 23, 1987, p. 45.

____. "Thanks for the Bonus, But Where's My Raise?" *U.S. News and World Report,* July 20, 1987, p. 43.

____. "You're Fired!" *U.S. News and World Report,* March 23, 1987, p. 50.

Brown, J. H. U. "The Consortium in Scientific Development." *Society of Research Administrators J.* (Winter 1978).

____. *The High Cost of Healing.* New York: Human Sciences Press, 1985.

____. "Medical Schools in Crisis." *Evaluation and the Health Professions* 11:147 (1988).

____. "The Research Consortium." *Research Management,* May 1981, p. 38.

Burke, T., A. Genn-Bash, and B. Haines. *Competition in Theory and Practice.* London: Croom Helm, 1988.

Carr, A. Z. "Is Business Bluffing Ethical?" *Harvard Business Review,* January 1968, p. 143.

"CEOs and Employees." *INC.,* November 1987, p. 70.

Cerullo, M. J. "Smoothing Management Information Flow with Systems Analysis." *Hospital Financial Management* 33 (8):12 (August 1979).

Christiansen, D. "Ethical Dilemmas Revisited." *IEEE Spectrum* 26 (4):21 (April 1989).

Chubb, J. E., and T. M. Moe. *Politics, Markets, and America's Schools.* Washington, D.C.: Brookings Institution, 1990.

Crawford, S. "Information and Communication among Scientists." *J. of the American Society for Information Science* 22:30 (1971).

Deming, W. E. *Sample Design in Business Research.* New York: John Wiley and Sons, 1960.

Deutsch, M. F. *Doing Business with the Japanese.* New York: New American Library, 1983.

Downs, A. *Inside Bureaucracy.* Boston: Little, Brown, 1967.

Drucker, P. "Some High Marks for American Management." *Wall Street J.,* August 17, 1981, p. 14.

Duchêne, F., and G. Shepherd. *Managing Industrial Change in Western Europe.* New York: Frances Pinter, 1987.

Dunnette, M. D., and E. A. Fleischman, eds. *Human Performance and Productivity.* Hillsdale, N.J.: Lawrence Erlbaum Associates, 1982.

Eason, K. D. "Patterns of Usage of a Flexible Information System." In *The Application of Information Technology,* edited by S. D. P. Harker and K. D. Eason. London: Taylor and Francis, 1990.

Ehrlich, P., and A. Ehrlich. "Speaking Out on Overpopulation." *Issues in Science and Technology* 5 (2):36 (Winter 1988–89).

Eisenberg, J. M., and A. J. Rosoff. "Physician Responsibility for the Cost of Unnecessary Medical Services." *New England J. of Medicine* 299:76 (1978).

England, R. "Ford Shifts Gears." *Insight,* July 13, 1987, p. 8.

Ewing, D. *The Managerial Mind.* New York: Free Press, 1964.

"Executive Compensation Scoreboard." *Business Week,* May 5, 1986, p. 59.

Fiedler, F. E., and M. M. Chemers. *Leadership and Effective Management.* Glenview, Ill.: Scott, Foresman, 1974.

"Ford Claims Honda Has Cost Advantage." *Houston Post,* August 24, 1987, p. 7F.

Fraley, A. E. *Schooling and Innovation.* New York: Tyler Gibson, 1981.

Friedman, M. M. *Three Major Factors in Business Management.* San Francisco: Social Sciences Reporters Conference (8th), 1958.

Fulmer, R. M. *The New Management.* 4th ed. New York: Macmillan, 1987.

Gabor, A. "What They Don't Teach You at Business School." *U.S. News and World Report,* July 13, 1987, p. 44.

Garvin, D. A. *Managing Quality.* New York: Free Press, 1988.

Ghiselli, E. E. *Explorations in Managerial Talent.* Pacific Palisades, Calif.: Goodyear, 1971.

Goldfarb, M., M. Hornbrook, and J. Rafferty. "Behavior of the Multiproduct Firm." *Medical Care* 18:185 (1980).

Grayson, C. J., Jr., and C. O'dell. *American Business, a Two-Minute Warning.* New York: Free Press, 1988.

Greenberg, D. "Can Chicken-Coop Inventors Help Us Win?" *U.S. News and World Report,* July 27, 1987, p. 42.

Griliches, Z. "R and D and Productivity." *Science* 237:31 (1987).

Guile, B. R., and J. B. Quinn, eds. *Managing Innovation.* Washington, D.C.: National Academy Press, 1988.

Halberstam, D. *The Reckoning.* New York: Avon Press, 1987.

Hall, E. T., and M. R. Hall. *Hidden Differences.* Garden City, N.Y.: Anchor Press/Doubleday, 1987.

Harari, O., and L. Mukai. "A New Decade Demands a New Breed of Manager." *Management Review,* August 1990, p. 20.

Hartman, C., and S. Pearlstein. "The Joy of Working." *INC.,* November 1987, p. 61.

"Health Care for an Aging Society." *Houston Law Review,* October 1989.

Ibe, K. "The Illusion of Japan as Invincible Economic Giant." *Wall Street J.,* September 21, 1981, p. 35.

Ikari, S. "The Japanese Work Ethic." *Sumitomo Corporation Bulletin,* Summer 1989.

Ishihara, S. *The Japan That Can Say No.* New York: Simon and Schuster, 1991.

Ivancevich, J. M., J. H. Donnelly, and J. L. Gibson. *Managing for Performance.* Dallas, Tex.: Business Publications, 1980.

Jarmul, D. "Will Cheaper Health Care Lead to Poorer Quality?" *National Research Council News Report* 37 (5):14 (May 1987).

Jason, H., and J. Westberg. *Teachers and Teaching in U.S. Medical Schools.* Norwalk, Conn.: Appleton-Century-Crofts, 1982.

Kanter, R. M. *Men and Women of the Corporation.* New York: Basic Books, 1977.

Karmin, M. W., et al. "Will the U.S. Stay Number One?" *U.S. News and World Report,* February 2, 1987, p. 18.

Kennedy, E. H. *Regulation of Clinical Laboratories: Hearings on S-1737.* Washington, D.C.: U.S. Government Printing Office, 1975.

Koestler, A. *The Ghost in the Machine.* New York: Macmillan, 1968.

Kolata, G. B. "Withholding Medical Treatment." *Science* 205:882 (1979).

Kraut, R. E., ed. *Technology and the Transformation of White-Collar Work.* Hillsdale, N.J.: Lawrence Erlbaum Associates, 1987.

Lederman, L. L. "Science and Technology Policies and Priorities." *Science* 237:1125 (1987).

Lehner, U. C. "Aid to Japan's Growth." *Wall Street J.,* September 14, 1981, p. 1.

Leth, S. *White Collar Productivity.* Houston, Tex.: American Productivity Center, 1985.

Lewis, J. D. "Technology, Enterprise, and American Economic Growth." *Science* 215:1204 (1982).

Ling, J. G., and G. D. Wallace. "Government-to-Industry Technology Transfer." *Bridge* 19 (3):21 (Fall 1989).

Longman, P. "Generational Equality." *Business and Health,* November 1986, p. 63.

McCormack, M. H. *What They Don't Teach You at Harvard Business School.* New York: Bantam Books, 1984.

McGinnis, J. M. "National Priorities in Disease Prevention." *Issues in Science and Technology* 5 (2):46 (Winter 1988–89).

Makihara, K. "Resigning — A Japanese Custom." *Houston Post,* August 9, 1987, p. 5E.

Marshall, E. "The Boom in Service Industries Will Not Solve U.S. Trade Problems." *Science* 237:243 (1987).

Miller, L. M. *Barbarians to Bureaucrats.* New York: Clarkson N. Potter, 1989.

Moore, T. "Personality Tests Are Back." *Fortune,* March 30, 1987, p. 74.

Morrison, E. F. "Cities in a Global Economy." *Issues in Science and Technology* 3 (4):42 (Summer 1987).

Murrin, T. J. "Thinking Globally, Acting Nationally." *Issues in Science and Technology* 6 (4):50 (Summer 1990).

National Academy of Engineering. *Design and Analysis of Integrated Manufacturing Systems.* Washington, D.C.: National Academy Press, 1988.

___. *The Technological Dimensions of International Competitiveness.* Washington, D.C.: National Academy Press, 1988.

National Center for Educational Statistics. *Digest of Educational Statistics.* Washington, D.C.: Department of Education; U.S. Government Printing Office, 1988.

National Research Council. *Everybody Counts.* Washington, D.C.: National Academy Press, 1989.

Neal, D. C., ed. *Consortia and Interinstitutional Cooperation.* London: Collier Macmillan, 1988.

Neuharth, A. *Confessions of an S.O.B.* New York: Doubleday, 1989.

Nielsen, R. P. "What Can Managers Do about Unethical Management?" *J. of Business Ethics* 6:309 (1987).

O'dell C. *Major Findings from People, Performance, and Pay.* Houston, Tex.: American Productivity and Quality Center, 1986.

Ohmae, K. "Japan vs. Japan: Only the Strong Survive." *Wall Street J.,* January 26, 1981, p. 20.

Osborne, D. "Refining State Technology Programs." *Issues in Science and Technology* 6 (4):55 (Summer 1990).

Ouchi, W. G. *Theory Z.* New York: Avon, 1982.

Packard, G. "Partners in Prosperity." *Atlantic Monthly,* May 1988, p. 41.

Parkinson, C. N. *Parkinson's Law.* New York: Ballantine Books, 1957.

Pascale, R. T., and A. G. Athos. *The Art of Japanese Management.* New York: Simon and Schuster, 1981.

Pauly, M. "What Is Unnecessary Surgery?" *Millbank Memorial Fund Quarterly* 57:95 (1979).

Porter, G. "Regaining Leadership through Industrial R and D." *National Academy of Engineering Reports,* December 1987, p. 23.

Post, J. E. "The Greening of Management." *Issues in Science and Technology* 6 (4):68 (Summer 1990).

Puri, T., and A. Bhide. "The Crucial Weaknesses of Japan Inc." *Wall Street J.,* June 6, 1981, p. 20.

R and D. Productivity. Culver City, Calif.: Hughes Aircraft, 1974.

Ramo, S. *The Business of Science.* New York: Hill and Wang, 1988.

Reisner, M. "The Next Water War." *Issues in Science and Technology* 5 (2):98 (Winter 1988–89).

"Responding to the Competitive Challenge: The Technological Dimension." *Bridge* 18 (1):3 (Spring 1988).

Robin, E. D. *Matters of Life and Death.* New York: W. H. Freeman, 1984.

Russell, L. B. *An Aging Population and the Use of Medical Care.* Washington, D.C.: Brookings Institution, 1981.

Sandroff, R. "How Ethical Is American Business?" *Working Woman,* September 1990, p. 113.

Sanoff, A. "A Watershed in the Workplace." *U.S. News and World Report,* May 30, 1988, p. 52.

Schumacher, E. F. *Small Is Beautiful.* New York: Harper and Row, 1973.

Schwartz, D. C., and J. M. Cooper. "Antitrust Policy and Technological Innovation." *Issues in Science and Technology* 1 (3):128 (Spring 1985).

Self, K. "Designing with Fuzzy Logic." *IEEE Spectrum* 27 (11):42 (November 1990).

Senia, A. "Companies Turn Old Ideas into Profits." *High Technology Business,* December 1987, p. 36.

Shapiro, I. "Second Thoughts about Japan." *Wall Street J.,* June 5, 1981, p. 24.

Sherrid, P. "America's Hottest New Export." *U.S. News and World Report,* July 27, 1987, p. 39.

Siu, R. G. H. *The Craft of Power.* New York: John Wiley and Sons, 1979.

Skrzycki, C., and M. Walsh. "America on the Auction Block." *U.S. News and World Report,* March 30, 1987, p. 56.

"Slave New World of the Machine." *Washington Post Weekly,* January 25, 1988, p. 6.

Smith, H. *The Power Game.* New York: Random House, 1988.

Sonnenstuhl, W. J., and H. M. Trice. *Strategies for Employee Assistance Programs.* Ithaca, N.Y.: ILR Press, 1986.

Spinrad, R. J. "Office Automation." *Science* 215:808 (1982).

Squires, A. M. "Maestros of Technology." *Invention and Technology,* Summer 1987, p. 24.

Stano, M. "Monopoly Power, Ownership Control, and Corporate Performance." *Bell J. of Economics* 7:672 (1976).

Stewart, C. T., Jr., and Y. Nihei. *Technology Transfer and Human Factors.* Lexington, Mass.: Lexington Books, 1987.

Sumney, L. W., and R. M. Burger. "Revitalizing the U.S. Semiconductor Industry." *Issues in Science and Technology* 3 (4):32 (Summer 1987).

Svoboda, F. "Borrowing Techniques from the Japanese." *Washington Post National Weekly,* January 4, 1988, p. 20.

Thurow, L. "A Weakness in Process Technology." *Science* 238:1659 (1987).

____. *The Zero-Sum Society.* New York: Basic Books, 1980.

Toffler, A. *Powershift.* New York: Bantam Books, 1990.

Tolchin, M., and S. Tolchin. *Buying into America.* New York: Times Books, 1988.

Topolnicki, D. M. "Your Stake in Local Schools." *Money* 19 (5):84 (May 1990).

Torrero, E. A. "R and D." *IEEE Spectrum* 27 (10), entire issue (October 1990).

University of Wisconsin. *Proceedings of the Conference on Research Consortia.* Madison, Wisconsin, November 10–11, 1988.

Visser, H., and E. Schoorl, eds. *Trade in Transit.* Boston: Kluwer Academic Publishers, 1987.

Weisner, J. "More R and D in the Right Places." *Issues in Science and Technology* 4 (1):13 (Fall 1987).

White House. *Final Report on Awards System Conference.* Washington, D.C.: U.S. Government Printing Office, 1984.

Wolf, M. J. *The Japanese Conspiracy.* New York: Empire Books, 1983.

Work, C. P., et al. "The 21st Century Executive." *U.S. News and World Report,* March 7, 1988, p. 48.

Zraket, C. A. "Dual-Use Technologies and National Coampetitiveness." *Bridge* 19 (3):14 (Fall 1989).

Index

About the Authors

J.H.U. BROWN is Professor of Biology at the University of Houston. He is the author or co-author of thirty books, primarily on biology, health care, and related subjects.

JACQUELINE COMOLA is Senior Vice President of the American Productivity and Quality Center in Houston, Texas. She is the author of *Improving Health Care Productivity*. She has also published numerous articles and presented many papers on employee training to various conferences.